Living in the Gap Between

PROMISE,
AND
REALITY

THE GOSPEL ACCORDING TO THE OLD TESTAMENT

A series of studies on the lives
of Old Testament characters, written for
laypeople and pastors, and designed to
encourage Christ-centered reading, teaching,
and preaching of the Old Testament.

TREMPER LONGMAN III
J. ALAN GROVES

Series Editors

Living in the Gap Between

PROMISE

AND

REALITY

THE GOSPEL ACCORDING TO

ABRAHAM

IAIN M. DUGUID

P&R

PUBLISHING

P.O. BOX 817 • PHILLIPSBURG • NEW JERSEY 08865-0817

Page design by Tobias Design
Typesetting by Michelle Feaster

Printed in the United States of America

Library of Congress Cataloging-in-Publication Data

Duguid, Iain M.
    Living in the gap between promise and reality : the Gospel according to Abraham / Iain M. Duguid.
        p.   cm. — (The Gospel according to the Old Testament)
    Includes bibliographical references and index.
    ISBN-10: 0-87552-652-7 (pbk.)
    ISBN-13: 978-0-87552-652-2 (pbk.)
    1. Abraham (Biblical patriarch) 2. Bible. O.T. Genesis, XI, 27–XXV, 18—Criticism, interpretation, etc. 3. Bible. O.T. Genesis, XI, 27–XXV, 18—Relation to the New Testament. 4. Bible. N.T.—Relation to Genesis, XI, 27–XXV, 18. I. Title. II. Series.
BS580.A3D84 1999
222'.1106—dc21   99–28877

*To the members of Redeemer Presbyterian Church,
Oxford (1992–95); with gratitude to God for our time
among you. May you always experience the full measure
of the joy of God's grace.*

CONTENTS

FOREWORD

The New Testament is in the Old concealed;
the Old Testament is in the New revealed.
—*Augustine*

Concerning this salvation, the prophets, who spoke of the grace that was to come to you, searched intently and with the greatest care, trying to find out the time and circumstances to which the Spirit of Christ in them was pointing when he predicted the sufferings of Christ and the glories that would follow. It was revealed to them that they were not serving themselves but you, when they spoke of the things that have now been told you by those who have preached the gospel to you by the Holy Spirit sent from heaven. Even angels long to look into these things. (1 Peter 1:10–12)

"In addition, some of our women amazed us. They went to the tomb early this morning but didn't find his body. They came and told us that they had seen a vision of angels, who said he was alive. Then some of our companions went to the tomb and found it just as the women had said, but him they did not see." He said to them, "How foolish you are, and how slow of heart to believe all that the prophets have spoken! Did not the Christ have to suffer these things and then enter his glory?" And beginning with Moses and all the Prophets, he explained to them what was said in all the Scriptures concerning himself. (Luke 24:22–27)

The prophets searched. Angels longed to see. And the disciples didn't understand. But Moses, the prophets, and all the Old Testament Scriptures had spoken about it— that Jesus would come, suffer, and then be glorified. God began to tell a story in the Old Testament, the ending for which the audience eagerly anticipated. But the Old Testament audience was left hanging. The plot was laid out but the climax was delayed. The unfinished story begged an ending. In Christ, God has provided the climax to the Old Testament story. Jesus did not arrive unannounced; his coming was declared in advance in the Old Testament, not just in explicit prophecies of the Messiah but by means of the stories of all of the events, characters, and circumstances on the Old Testament. God was telling a larger, overarching, unified story. From the account of creation in Genesis to the final stories of the return from exile, God progressively unfolded his plan of salvation. And the Old Testament account of that plan always pointed in some way to Christ.

AIMS OF THIS SERIES

The Gospel According to the Old Testament Series is committed to the proposition that the Bible, both Old and New Testaments, is a unified revelation of God, and that its thematic unity is found in Christ. The individual books of the Old Testament exhibit diverse genres, styles, and individual theologies, but tying them all together is the constant foreshadowing of, and pointing forward to, Christ. Believing in the fundamentally Christocentric nature of the Old Testament, as well as the New Testament, we offer this series of studies in the Old Testament with the following aims:

- to lay out the pervasiveness of the revelation of Christ in the Old Testament
- to promote a Christ-centered reading of the Old Testament
- to encourage Christ-centered preaching and teaching from the Old Testament

To this end, the volumes in this series are written for pastors and laypeople, not scholars.

While such a series could take a number of different shapes, we have decided, in most cases, to focus individual volumes on Old Testament figures—people—rather than books or themes. Some books, of course, will receive major attention in connection with their authors or main characters (e.g., Daniel or Isaiah). Also, themes will be emphasized in connection with particular figures.

It is our hope and prayer that this series will revive interest in and study of the Old Testament as readers recognize that the Old Testament points forward to Jesus Christ.

TREMPER LONGMAN III
J. ALAN GROVES

ACKNOWLEDGMENTS

N o book could be written without the assistance and encouragement of numerous people. The temptation in writing this page, as with the acceptance speeches of Oscar-winning actors, is to try to give a complete listing of all those "without whom this would not have been possible." Such a list would try the patience of reader and publisher alike, while still inevitably missing someone. So I will endeavor to be brief.

This book originated as a series of sermons preached at Redeemer Presbyterian Church, Oxford, England; they were then updated and re-delivered in a very different setting during a pastoral vacancy at Aliso Creek Presbyterian Church in Laguna Niguel, California. I want to thank both congregations of God's people for their encouragement and support. The series editors, Al Groves and Tremper Longman III, were also my teachers at Westminster Seminary in Philadelphia; I therefore owe them a double debt. Thanks are due to Jim Scott and Thom Notaro at P&R Publishing for improving the readability of the manuscript in numerous ways. The faults and shortcomings, however, remain my own.

I would particularly like to thank my wife, Barb, my most faithful and enthusiastic critic. She field-tested the material in a women's Bible study at New Life Presbyterian Church in Escondido, California, and contributed many of the questions in the "For Further Reflection" sections. Without her love and constant support, I wouldn't have nearly as much fun doing what I do. Thanks are also due to my children, Jamie, Sam, Hannah, Robbie, and Rosie for keeping me firmly in touch with real life and reminding me of the things that are most important.

This book is dedicated, however, to the memory of Redeemer Presbyterian Church, Oxford (1992–95). No fledgling pastor could ever have had a more loving and committed congregation. Of each member it could be said, as Paul said of Timothy, that they took a genuine interest in the welfare of one another and the wider community, not putting their own interests first, but those of Jesus Christ (Phil. 3:20–21). Barb and I praise God for every remembrance of you all, and look forward to our reunion in heaven, when the full fruit of your labors will be revealed.

SOLI DEO GLORIA

INTRODUCTION:
LIVING IN
THE REALITY GAP

How do you respond when you find yourself falling into the reality gap? How do you feel when there seems to be a huge difference between what God has promised and what you see now? What do you do when the vision you once had of the way your life was supposed to work out seems to be crumbling into dust? It is easy to be a Christian in the sunshine of Palm Sunday, surrounded by the crowds chanting their praises to Jesus, "Hosanna! Blessed is he who comes in the name of the Lord!" But it is much harder to be a disciple in the gathering gloom on the road to Emmaus, puzzling over the death of the Messiah and not yet seeing how that death will lead to resurrection.

For most of us, much of our life seems to be spent trudging along that dreary road to Emmaus. For one person, the reality gap may appear in the form of sudden and unexpected unemployment, with little prospect of another job. For another, it may come with sickness and crippling health problems. It may come to you through the death of a spouse or child. It may be caused by an intense frustration with the church in which God has placed you. Any or all of these circumstances may cause a crisis of faith in your life as you ponder the reality gap between what God has promised and the circumstances in which you find yourself. *Surely this isn't what life should be like as a Christian,* you think to yourself.

THE EMMAUS ROAD SERMON

Where can you turn when you experience a crisis of faith? What help is available to strengthen the faith of those who are caught in the reality gap, who feel stuck in a time warp along the road between Jerusalem and Emmaus? Perhaps the best reply to that question is the answer that Jesus himself gave to the disciples who first traveled along that dark road. After they recounted their puzzlement to him, not yet realizing who he was, Jesus responded,

> "How foolish you are, and how slow of heart to believe all that the prophets have spoken! Did not the Christ have to suffer these things and then enter his glory?" And beginning with Moses and all the Prophets, he explained to them what was said in all the Scriptures concerning himself. (Luke 24:25–27)

In other words, Jesus gave them an Old Testament sermon that started with the writings of Moses (the first five books of the Bible) and continued through all the prophets (the rest of the Old Testament), showing them how the pattern of suffering followed by glory is continually interwoven through the threads of the history of God's people. If they had understood the Old Testament better, the death and resurrection of Jesus would not have come as such a shock. They would have been better equipped to face the tough realities of life with an unshakable faith in God.

ABRAHAM AS OUR EXAMPLE

Where did Abraham fit into that Emmaus road sermon? Luke doesn't tell us the details, but it is hard to imagine that Abraham was overlooked by Jesus. Abraham is supremely the man of faith in the Old Testament. He, perhaps more than almost any other person in the Bible, knew what it means to live by faith in the face of overwhelming circumstances. In the pages of the book of Genesis, we find recorded for us the faith, and the failures, of a man like us, who lived in the gap between promise and reality.

Indeed, even in the Old Testament, Abraham was regarded as an exemplary figure. In Isaiah 51:2, the exiles in Babylon were urged to consider his experience as a model for their own: "Look to Abraham, your father, and to Sarah, who gave you birth. When I called him he was but one, and I blessed him and made him many." Just as Abraham had been called by God from the city of Ur, against overwhelming odds, to enter the Promised Land, so also the exiles could rely on God to fulfill his promises to the patriarch. They could have faith that the God of Abraham would return them once again to that land, impossible though that seemed.

But the use of Abraham as an example goes back further than the Exile. As we examine the narrative of Abraham, we shall find that his story was written to provide encouragement for the generation in the wilderness, those who were on an Emmaus journey of their own, stuck in the reality gap between their calling out of Egypt by God and their still-future possession of the Land of Promise. For them, too, Abraham provided both an example to follow and a warning to avoid sin. The fertility of Egypt was a sidetrack for Abraham, just as it was for them; the temptation to take shortcuts and "help God out" was very real for both; Abraham's call to exercise faith in the unseen reality of God's promise against all odds was a challenge for them to heed.

But what about us? We do not live in the wilderness of Sinai, nor among the exiles of Babylon. What can we learn from Abraham? The writer to the Hebrews gives us our answer in Hebrews 3–4 by showing us the fundamental analogy between our present spiritual position as Christians and that of the wilderness generation. We too have not yet entered our rest (4:6). We too run the risk of disobeying the gospel promise and falling short of God's blessing (3:12; 4:1). Although everything in creation is subject to the authority of Jesus, at present we often do not see that heavenly reality clearly reflected in our own earthly experience (Heb. 2:8). We need to live by faith, just like our Old Testament forefathers (Heb. 11). So we too can learn a great deal from Abraham's example of how to live in the gap between promise and reality.

ABRAHAM AND THE GOSPEL

Yet if Abraham is only an example for us to follow, we are of all men most to be pitied. Who among us can live up to the standard of even a flawed hero such as Abraham? Thankfully, our salvation as Christians rests not on our trying to do what Abraham did, but on the sacrifice of Christ on the cross in our place, whereby our sins were atoned for, the wrath of God was turned away from us, and we were reconciled to him. To put it another way, the gospel is not "What would Abraham do?" but "What has Jesus done?" So, in our exposition of the life of Abraham, we will see not only how he provides positive and negative examples for us, but also how he acts as a forerunner and shadow, pointing forward to Christ.

This is, after all, the central thrust of the Emmaus road sermon. Jesus recounted for his disciples what Moses and the prophets had written, not because they were full of good examples for them to follow, but because they spoke of him. Specifically, they spoke of his sufferings and the glories that would follow. The whole Old Testament is thereby declared to be a thoroughly Christocentric book. This is true, not simply because there are superficial parallels between certain Old Testament events and events in the life of Jesus, but more profoundly because the whole Old Testament was designed by God to provide a context within which to understand the sufferings and glorification of Christ. Our greatest need, in order to live by faith in the midst of the reality gap, is not to have a good example to follow. Rather, we need a growing understanding of the gospel of Jesus Christ, of his sufferings and the glory that followed, as the context for our present sufferings and certain hope for the glory to come.

I

THE PREPARATION

OF A SAINT

(GENESIS 11:27−32)

The making of a tennis player does not begin the first time he or she steps onto Centre Court at Wimbledon; nor does the making of a concert violinist begin on stage at Carnegie Hall. Such careers begin much earlier than that, often in childhood. Making it to the top demands sacrificing much that others take for granted; while others play, they must work—on lobs and smashes, serves and backhands, scales and arpeggios, bowing and fingering. Without those years of preparation, they would never be ready for their big moment in the public eye, the goal to which their whole life has been heading. Indeed, it would be unfair to expect a top performance at the highest level from a beginner. Only those who have matured through long and sometimes tedious years of preparation are equipped to undertake such a searching test.

The same principle holds true in God's service. Like an astute coach or a gifted teacher, God prepares his saints for the tasks to which he has appointed them before he uses them. Moses, for example, spent forty years in the desert, herding sheep, before God called him to lead his people out of Egypt. What better preparation in patience could there have been for his assignment of leading an equally stubborn flock of people through the wilderness for forty years? Similarly, David learned courage from his own experience as a shepherd. Later, the one who had learned how to take on wild animals in the defense of his flock would be called upon to take on the biggest wild animal of all, mighty Goliath, in the defense of God's flock. God knows how to prepare his people for the tasks to which they are assigned.

THE PREPARATION OF ABRAHAM AND SARAH

The principle of preparation for service is also evident in the life of Abraham. We often miss this aspect of Abraham's story because we usually commence our reading of it at the beginning of Genesis 12. But that's not actually where his story begins. In the book of Genesis, the beginning of a major new section is frequently marked by the formula "This is the account of. . . ." So, for example, we find "This is the account of Noah" (Gen. 6:9), "This is the account of Abraham's son Isaac" (25:19), and "This is the account of Jacob" (37:2). Abraham's story is introduced by the same marker at Genesis 11:27: "This is the account of Terah." We tend to skip over the verses that follow this announcement in order to get into the exciting material of Genesis 12. After all, aren't the intervening verses only about obscure genealogies and incidental details, which may be of interest to Old Testament experts but have nothing to say to ordinary people? By no means! In fact, quite the reverse is true. Genesis 11:27–32 gives us vital information about the background to the calling and subsequent career of Abraham.

You see, God's dealings with Abraham didn't start with him as a seventy-five-year-old about to set out on a journey to Canaan. God didn't just slip down to Haran, looking for a suitable retiree to act as the father of his people. No, he had been preparing Abraham for a while—even though he (or Abram, as he was then known) was quite unaware of that fact. The circumstances are recorded for us in Genesis 11:31-32.

> Terah took his son Abram, his grandson Lot son of Haran, and his daughter-in-law Sarai, the wife of his son Abram, and together they set out from Ur of the Chaldeans to go to Canaan. But when they came to Haran, they settled there. Terah lived 205 years, and he died in Haran.

We find out here that it was actually Abram's father, Terah, who first set out for Canaan, taking Abram with him. The Scriptures don't tell us why he wanted to make the move. This was a period of history in which there were great movements of population around the Middle East. Terah, Abram, and Lot would by no means have been alone in pulling up stakes and setting off in search of greener pastures. But they never made it to Canaan. For some reason—again, we're not told why—they stopped at Haran and settled there. Yet the idea of going to Canaan had been planted in Abram's mind. Through this experience of moving once from home and family in Ur, he was being prepared by God, so that when the call came to get up and move on to Canaan, he was ready. God had fitted him to hear his call and answer it. In an unexpected way, God was preparing his saint for future service.

Of course, Terah himself was not picked at random, either. The genealogy of Genesis 11:10-26 shows us that he came from the line of Shem, the son of Noah. He was a descendant of the very line in which God had been working for many generations. What is more, in the genealogies of Genesis 5 and 11:10-26, it is the tenth name that is the one of key significance. Noah, the one in whom the line of Adam was preserved through the Flood, was the tenth patriarch in the line from Adam. Abram was the tenth patriarch in the line of Shem, suggesting that through Abram a new deliverance would be set in motion.

God's plan from the beginning was to preserve for himself a godly line, through whom the promise of a redemptive offspring of Eve (Gen. 3:15) would ultimately be granted. God planned that this "seed" of the woman would ultimately triumph over Satan and his cohorts. This godly line was soon endangered from without and within. Angered by the acceptance of his brother's offering, Cain killed his brother, Abel (Gen. 4:8). But God responded by giving Eve another child, or, more literally, "another seed" (4:25). When humanity became utterly corrupt within a few generations, God kept Noah safe through the Flood, so that the line of promise could continue (Gen. 6–9). Then, with Abram, came the next phase in the history of redemption. Although Abram may have been unaware of the ways in which God had prepared him for his task, everything was ready.

Sarah (or Sarai, as her parents had named her) too was being prepared in the school of hard knocks for women. Genesis 11:30 tells us, "Now Sarai was barren." And then the writer repeats himself (just in case you missed it the first time around): "She had no children." Not to be able to have children in a society where a woman's value was measured by her fertility was a bitter blow indeed. Sarai must have shed many bitter tears over her inability to bear children. But, paradoxically, her inability in this area was a crucial part of God's preparation of her for her role in his plan. In order for her to be the mother of the child of promise, it was necessary for her to be unable to bear children *without* the direct intervention of God.

OUR PREPARATION

In Ephesians 2:10, Paul describes us as "God's workmanship, created in Christ Jesus to do good works, which God prepared in advance for us to do." That raises the question, "For what good works is God preparing you?" Your answer right now may well be, "I haven't a clue." God's purposes are certainly not always transparent at the time. Moses probably had no idea why he was stuck in the desert with the sheep. He must have felt permanently sidelined. Likewise, David had little idea of the future greatness for which he was being fitted. Abram could scarcely have discerned the higher hand bringing him from Ur to Haran, and Sarai's tears were not answered with an explanation of the need for her present pain. Only later, with the benefit of hindsight, would they be able to look back and discern how God had indeed done all things well in their lives. In the meantime, they simply had to cling to God, believing, though not understanding.

An awareness of the way in which God frequently works may similarly provide a vital perspective on our own experience. The situation in which we find ourselves may well be a key part of God's preparation of us for the task to which he will call us at some point in the future. But it may be only as we look back that we will come to understand how it all works into God's plan for our lives. In the meantime, we may simply have to cling to God, believing, though not understanding.

AN EXAMPLE

Let me give a small example from my own experience. When I felt God calling me to the ministry at the age of seventeen, a vital part of that call was Romans 15:20, where Paul proclaims, "It has always been my ambition to preach the gospel." As a teenager, God impressed that verse upon my heart as a call to me personally to share Paul's ambition. Over the years, however, I came to recognize that I had latched onto only half of what Paul is really saying. His full statement is, "It has always been my ambition to preach the gospel where Christ was not known, so that I would not be building on someone else's foundation."

In other words, what Paul is actually proclaiming is not so much his commitment to preaching the gospel as his commitment to church planting. This fact came home to me only as I sat in front of a congregation of people, about to tell them that the Lord was apparently opening the doors for us to go to Oxford, England, to plant a church there. I almost fell off my chair when I made the connection! What we had considered to be the outcome of a series of strange twists and turns in our lives, when we had frequently been unsure of what the long-term future held, now seemed to have been in the Lord's mind all along, even though we had had no idea of it! What a comfort it was then, and throughout our time in Oxford, to be assured that God had brought us there for his purposes.

It may be the same for you, too. The experiences in which you find yourself now may very well turn out to be God's preparing of you for the good works he has planned for you to do later. That's a great encouragement, isn't it? Of course, a caution is necessary at this point: we must not elevate our reading of God's working through circumstances into authoritative guidance; we can easily be wrong! We must not forget that the Bible is the only infallible rule in our lives. No matter how clear the Lord's leading may seem to us, we are still called upon to subject our understanding of it to the Scriptures and also to the wisdom and discernment of the wider body of Christ. But when circumstances do work together to point us in a particular direction, or to show us how

God has indeed worked things together for our good, we should take encouragement from them and thank the Lord for them.

Praise God that he prepares his people through many different circumstances before he calls them to any task! By the way, that's not just a lesson for young people to learn. Moses and Abram were still in their preparation stage long after most people have retired!

PREPARATION DOES NOT GUARANTEE "SUCCESS"

But even lengthy preparation does not guarantee immediate success. Although God prepared Abram and Sarai to hear his call, and then called them to become a great nation through which blessing would come to all nations, for a long time all that distinguished them from their neighbors was the promise of God. There was no halo of glory surrounding their camels as they traveled from Haran to Canaan; nor was there a pillar of cloud and fire to lead them, as Israel had coming out of Egypt. At a time when many other people were traversing the Near East, they appeared to be just another group of travelers. Only the promise of God marked them out.

It's the same way today, isn't it? What marks you out from your non-Christian neighbors? You're not smarter than they are; you're not richer; you're not better looking or healthier. You experience many of the same kinds of problems and crises that they do. So what marks you out as different? Only the promises of God do. If you're a Christian, you know that God is working in you and through you to achieve his purposes in the world. If you're a Christian, you know that "in all things God works for the good of those who love him" (Rom. 8:28).

It is precisely that promise which enables you to experience the reality gap. For the non-Christian, there is logically no reality gap. His or her life may be going well or it may not, but either way it has no meaning. If one is simply a chance collocation of atoms, there is no reason why one's life should go well or why one's sufferings should have any significance. There is no promise that the non-Christian can claim. He or she is left simply hoping against hope that everything will turn out all right in the end. The Christian, however, is different. He or she knows that God is in control of all things and that, even if all appearances are to the contrary, God has a plan in which all things in heaven and under heaven will work out for his glory and our good. It is precisely our faith that creates the reality gap when we don't understand how particular trials or circumstances will work out.

STAYING STRONG IN THE REALITY GAP

So how do you stay strong in the midst of the reality gap, when you find yourself drowning in painful feelings, dire circumstances, or broken relationships? The answer is simple—at least in theory. You cling to the promises of God and the God of the promises. You don't have to understand; you just have to cling. That is the lesson that Abraham had to learn. Like so many of us, he had to learn the lesson not once, not twice, but repeatedly. It took him a while to catch on. But we have an advantage over Abraham. We have the whole history of God's faithful dealings with his people, recorded in the Scriptures for our instruction. What is more, God's promises to us have been signed and sealed in the broken body and shed blood of Christ. Abraham had to leave his home and his family on the strength of the bare word of God's call. We have this further assurance: "[God] did not spare his own Son, but gave him up for us all—how will he not also, along with him, graciously give us all things?" (Rom. 8:32).

That is why it is such an encouragement to gather around the Lord's Table. We come as those who are marked out from the world by the promises of God and by faith partake of the sign and seal of the promise. There we remember that Christ died for us. We remember that there is no forgiveness anywhere else, nor do we need any other resource. There we remember that Jesus Christ is coming back to bring us to his heavenly home, where we will gather at another feast in his presence, when the gap between promise and reality will finally be closed once and for all. There we worship in awe at God's stubborn grace, his inexplicable love for sinners, whom he slowly, patiently, and thoroughly turns into saints who can stand forever in his presence.

FOR FURTHER REFLECTION

1. How would the fact that Abram had already set out once for Canaan make obedience to God's call easier when it came?
2. How did God prepare the following characters in biblical history for their place in his plans: Joseph (Gen. 37–46), Moses (Ex. 2–14), David (1 Sam. 16–20), Esther (Est. 2–4), and Paul (Acts 7:54–9:31)?
3. How has God prepared you for the work he has given you to do?
4. What might God be doing in your life right now to prepare you for his service in the future?
5. Are you sometimes afraid of what God may ask you to do? If so, why?
6. How does this passage of Scripture encourage you to trust God more?

2

BELIEVING
THE UNBELIEVABLE
(GENESIS 12)

The letter began, "Iain Duguid, you may have won $25 million." I think the letter then went on to give me some suggestions as to how I might spend my newfound wealth. I don't really remember, however, because I threw the letter straight into the bin. Some things are just too good to be true. Some promises are too farfetched for a skeptic like me to believe. So I find myself wondering how Abram responded when God spoke to him in these terms:

> I will make you into a great nation
>   and I will bless you;
> I will make your name great,
>   and you will be a blessing.
> I will bless those who bless you,
>   and whoever curses you I will curse;
> and all peoples on earth
>   will be blessed through you. (Gen. 12:2–3)

The Bible doesn't tell us the thoughts that went through Abram's head. It doesn't reveal how he broke the news to his wife. He simply obeyed. God spoke—and Abram went. Just as in the very beginning of all things, in those first days of creation, when God simply spoke the word and it happened, so also here, in this new beginning for mankind, God spoke the word and it came to pass.

A NEW BEGINNING FOR MANKIND

Make no mistake, what we see here in Genesis 12 is nothing short of a new beginning for mankind. In the first eleven chapters of Genesis, we observe the slow, steady, shocking spread of sin from its origin in the Garden of Eden. Five times in these chapters, God's solemn curse is pronounced upon sin and sinners, replacing the original blessing upon life in the Garden. But now God begins the process of re-creating for himself a people by pronouncing a fivefold blessing upon Abram. God will bless Abram and turn him into the very embodiment of blessing, a living model of what blessing should be. In the same way that Babe Ruth is "Mr. Baseball," Abram will be "Mr. Blessing." What the builders of the Tower of Babel sought to do in their own behalf and failed to accomplish—to establish a lasting city and thus make a name for themselves—God will do for Abram. God will make him into a nation and make his name great. Through his obedience, Abram will bring blessing to the whole world: "All peoples on earth will be blessed through you." God's original plan of blessing for the whole world will be brought to fruition through Abram's obedience. The way of blessing that was once marked by the Tree of Life and then by Noah's ark is now marked by identification with Abram and his seed. Abram is promised a heady mixture of power, prestige, and status.

That blessing will be worked out through Abram's becoming "a great nation" (12:2). Implicit in this promise is what becomes explicit later in the narrative, that God will grant Abraham descendants and a land for them to live in. Indeed, in large measure the story of the Pentateuch is the working out of these promises of blessing, descendants, and land.

There are fundamental obstacles along the road to the fulfillment of each promise. How can sinners enjoy God's blessing? How can an elderly and barren couple have descendants? How can a handful of people possess a land that is already occupied by others? From a human perspective, the obstacles seem insuperable. But, as the Pentateuch unfolds, it becomes clear that nothing can stand in the way of the purposes of the sovereign and omnipotent God, who called heaven and earth into being out of nothing.

YOUR VISION IS TOO SMALL

Big promises make big demands on your faith, don't they? They demand a big vision. Given the choice, Abram would probably have settled for forty acres of prime real estate. He would have been content with enough land for himself and his immediate family to live on. But God didn't ask Abram what he wanted. He sovereignly chose to give him an entire country—far more land than he could ever have needed himself. God gave to Abram the whole land—north, south, east, and west—as far as the eye could see (Gen. 13:14–15).

Similarly, Abram would quite happily have settled for one son, even the offspring of his wife's servant, Hagar. You can see that from Abram's reaction when God tells him in Genesis 17 that Sarah is going to have a son. He laughs to himself and says, "If only Ishmael might live under your blessing!" (Gen. 17:18). Abram was really saying, "God, that's too difficult. Let's just settle for something a little more reasonable, shall we?" A son for

Sarah at their age was just too much to hope for. But God didn't want simply to give him a son by his wife's servant; he wanted to give him countless descendants of his very own, as many as the stars of the sky or the dust of the earth. He didn't want simply to give Abram enough property for him to be comfortable on; he wanted him to possess the whole land. Abram's vision was too small! God wanted to do something big with him.

What about you? Are you settling for a vision that is too small in your life? Are you choosing the easy option because you don't really believe God can bring about something great in your life? Yes, God sometimes calls us to be faithful in the little things, but is that *really* your calling, or are you afraid to hope for anything more? And what about your church? Do you expect to see God do great things there? Do you pray for God to do great things there, or are you content just to survive? All too often we don't really expect God to do anything dramatic, do we? It all seems too difficult to imagine. Yet we are part of an army with a great commission. We have received our marching orders to take the gospel to the ends of the earth: "Go and make disciples of all nations" (Matt. 28:19). Along with those instructions comes the divine promise: "And surely I am with you always, to the very end of the age" (v. 20). If God is with us, then what task is impossible? Like Abram, you and I need to hear the challenge posed by God's promises.

THE WAY OF GREATNESS

Abram embarked on the way of greatness by following the path of self-sacrifice. The man through whom the promised salvation of the world was to come had first of all to be isolated from all that he held dear. He had to leave his home and his family, his friends and his relatives. In addition, he had to leave the centers of power in the world. Ur and Haran were two of the three greatest centers of trade in Mesopotamia at that time. They were the New York and Los Angeles of the ancient world, the places where the movers and shakers lived. He had to leave all of that behind and go—but where? He was not told the destination right away. He was simply told to go "to the land I will show you" (Gen. 12:1). If he had been told what his destination was, would he have been excited by the news? Not likely. He was going to take possession of a backward land with the dubious distinction of being regularly overrun and fought over by invading armies. But God spoke, and Abram went.

Upon arrival, Abram's first concern was to travel over the length and breadth of the land, setting up altars and calling on the name of the Lord. Only three sites are mentioned: Shechem (12:6), the area between Bethel and Ai (v. 8), and the Negev (v. 9). These were the places that Jacob later visited on his return to the Promised Land in Genesis 34–35, and they were key sites in the conquest of the land under Joshua. In setting up altars at these places, Abram was laying claim to the land as belonging to his God. But he was also doing what the godly line had persistently done in Genesis 1–11. In Genesis 4:26, we read that in the time of Seth's son Enosh, men began to call on the name of the Lord; and we know that people offered sacrifices as early as the days of Cain and Abel. The builders of the Tower of Babel may have done neither of these things, but Abram was of a different stock. For him, worship was essential and natural.

FAITH OVERWHELMED BY CIRCUMSTANCES

However, Abram soon found himself overwhelmed by circumstances and turned his back on that land. "Now there was a famine in the land" (Gen. 12:10). It's a simple statement, but one full of foreboding. After all, this was the Land of Promise. Might Abram not reasonably have expected it to be a land flowing with milk and honey? But hardly had he pitched his tent when he found the land unable to support him and his small family. What hope was there, then, for the great nation the Lord had promised that he would become? Abram's faith was at once put to the test—and he faltered.

Have you had that experience? You start out on something, convinced it is God's will. You have high hopes at the beginning. But almost before you have begun, the whole project seems to start falling apart. None of your hopes are realized. The whole situation is a mess, and you wonder whether it could really have been God's leading that you followed. Surely we can identify with Abram's failure.

GOING DOWN TO EGYPT

So it is that we find Abram going down to Egypt. In the Old Testament, going to Egypt is frequently the alternative to trusting in the Lord. Thus, when the children of Israel were wandering in the wilderness and were assailed by hunger, instead of trusting in the Lord to provide food, they moaned about their memories of the "fleshpots" of Egypt. And when the Lord provided manna, they remembered the variety of Egypt's foodstuffs—the fish, the cucumbers, the melons, the leeks, the garlic. Egypt, dependent as it was upon the regular rise and fall of the Nile, rather than the irregularities of rainfall, was the natural port to turn to in a storm such as that in which Abram found himself.

Going down to Egypt was a natural choice, but not necessarily a wise one. For immediately God's whole promise was placed in jeopardy. Not only was Abram willing to give up—at least temporarily—his claim to the Land of Promise, but he also placed at risk the promised descendants who would occupy the land. He did this by making his wife, Sarai, pretend that she was his sister. Again, it seemed the natural thing to do. It was, after all, not completely untrue, for Sarai was his half-sister (Gen. 20:12). Abram was afraid, not entirely without reason, that the whole truth might cost him his life. If his fears had been realized, he would not have been the only person in the Old Testament to be conveniently disposed of in order to allow the king to add a new wife to his harem (see 2 Sam. 11). And then what would have become of the promise?

But Abram's logic, natural as it was, was fatally flawed. He had forgotten that the God whom he served was greater than his problems. He thought that God needed some help in fulfilling his promise. He thought too much about the potential disasters that might befall him and too little about obeying God and letting the chips fall where they may. Isn't that what we do so often? We ask, "What if this were to happen? What if things don't work out? What if I lose my job for telling the truth? What if I don't get that promotion because I wasn't willing to put in the extra hours, because I wanted to spend more time with my family?" Well, what about it?

Far from safeguarding the promise, Abram's crafty strategy nearly destroyed the whole plan. Abram was gone from the Promised Land, Sarai was lost to Pharaoh's harem, and instead of Abram's being a blessing to the nations, the Lord inflicted serious diseases on Pharaoh and his household because of what Abram had done. As Oliver Hardy used to say to Stan Laurel, "That's another fine mess you've got us into." Oh, in one sense the plan worked beautifully. Abram got rich out of it, acquiring a good selection of animals and servants (Gen. 12:16). Everybody would favor the brother of the king's newest wife. But, at the same time, what thoughts were going through Abram's mind? Could earthly prosperity make up for having apparently wrecked God's plan? I hardly think so. Those who turn their back on God's call in favor of what this world has to offer often live to lament their choice. Yet having once made the decision, Abram could not undo it.

Thanks be to God, however, that his plans are not so easily thwarted. The God who called the universe into existence at the snap of his fingers was not to be foiled by the blunderings of his human helpers. Circumstances, folly, and even sin would not stand in the way of God's purpose to make Abram a great blessing. What a comforting thought that is to all of us! How often we start out with good motives, yet quickly get sidetracked by our own incompetence or fear. We botch opportunities to share our faith. We compromise our holy lifestyle, under pressure to conform and be like others. Yet above and beyond it all, God's purpose stands secure. This is not an excuse for us to be lazy or to fudge difficult situations. The Lord would bring Abram back through this particular test over and over again, as someone teaching a horse to jump always brings it back to the fence at which it balks until finally the horse jumps it. Abram would finally learn that God is able to fulfill his promise on his own, without Abram's help.

GENESIS 12 AND JESUS CHRIST

Genesis 12 is not just about Abram's successes and failures. It also points forward to the coming of Christ. The key to making the connection is found in Galatians 3:16, where Paul says this:

> The promises were spoken to Abraham and to his seed. The Scripture does not say "and to seeds," meaning many people, but "and to your seed," meaning one person, who is Christ.

In other words, according to Paul, the promises made to Abram already have Christ in view. When God says to Abram in Genesis 12:7, "To your offspring [*lit.*, seed] I will give this land," he is talking about Christ. In other words, Abram functions as a miniature picture, a representation of Christ ahead of time. Do you see how this opens up a whole new perspective on this passage? Did Abram leave home and family to go to a backward nation at God's command? Jesus did more than that. He left the Father's side in heaven to come to earth, to an insignificant town in a second-rate state, where he lived unnoticed for thirty years (Phil. 2:6–8). What is more, like Abram, he did so on the strength of God's promise. He is the one to whom the messianic promise of Psalm 2 is addressed: "Ask of me, and I will make the nations your inheritance, the ends of the earth your possession. You will rule them with an iron scepter; you will dash them to pieces like pottery" (v. 9).

Abram received a great name, and was a blessing to those who blessed him, while those who cursed him were cursed. But Christ has received "the name that is above every name," that "at the name of Jesus every knee should bow" (Phil. 2:9–10). Those who come to Christ and are incorporated into him receive in him every spiritual blessing (Eph. 1). However, what do the Scriptures say about those who curse Christ? According to Matthew 25:41–43,

> Then he will say to those on his left, "Depart from me, you who are cursed, into the eternal fire prepared for the devil and his angels. For I was hungry and you gave me nothing to eat, I was thirsty and you gave me nothing to drink, I was a stranger and you did not invite me in, I needed clothes and you did not clothe me, I was sick and in prison and you did not look after me."

Those who despise Christ, who treat him as someone who can safely be ignored, will be numbered among the cursed.

THE WAY OF GREATNESS FOR JESUS

Like Abram, Jesus Christ found that following the way of promise took him through the reality gap. The one who was promised the nations of the earth as his inheritance came to his own people, and they did not receive him (John 1:11). The exalted Son of Man, pictured in Daniel 7 as sitting on the seat of judgment, was himself judged by the Sanhedrin and condemned to death. But, unlike Abraham, who told a lie to save his own life, Jesus told the truth, knowing it would cost him his life, so that our unrighteous lives might be saved. The one who was promised that he would rule the nations with a rod of iron was himself scourged by Roman soldiers on that first Good Friday. The only sinless one was given a criminal's death, lifted up on the cross, a fate that the law regarded as a sign of God's judgment. The light of the world hung under a darkened sky, the sun itself being ashamed to witness such a travesty of justice. If ever there was a man in the reality gap, it was Jesus. Abram's experience points us forward to the sufferings of Christ.

But did the promise of God falter that day? By no means! On the contrary, that first Easter was the key to the fulfillment of God's promises, all of which find their yes and amen in Christ. Was it a travesty of justice? On a human level, yes. But on God's level, it was a display of divine justice! Sin was condemned and judged most severely, yet sinners themselves are redeemed, bought back for God. The sinless one was made sin, so that we, the sinful ones, might be made holy. He was pierced for my transgressions; he was crushed for my iniquities; the punishment that brought me peace was upon him; by his wounds I am healed (Isa. 53).

In the Resurrection, the reality gap was bridged once and for all. There the firstfruits of the glories that would follow Christ's sufferings were revealed. He arose in glorious form; so also shall those who trust in him rise in glory. He ascended to the right hand of the Father; so also shall those who trust in him surely rise to new life in the Father's presence. Even now, the nations around the globe are being brought into his kingdom, with men and women from the North and the South and the East and the West beginning to confess Christ as Lord.

LIVING IN THE LIGHT OF EASTER

In the meantime, you and I continue to live here and now in the reality gap. Today our thoughts may be firmly fixed on Easter Sunday, but tomorrow is another Monday. Like Abraham, we have received the great and precious promises of God, and strive to believe them in the face of the overwhelming disappointments of life. We find ourselves struggling with the temptation to abandon the promises in favor of the apparently abundant provisions of Egypt.

The solution is to cling to the promises of God and to the God of the promises. Look to the risen Christ, who guarantees the fulfillment of the promises. Follow after him, remembering that our lives are patterned after his: first suffering, then glory. As Jesus himself reminds us, "In this world you will have trouble. But take heart! I have overcome the world" (John 16:33). *Trouble, famine, hardship, wilderness, exile*—these are the biblical words that describe our present existence. It's not a picnic. It was never intended to be a picnic. We are pilgrims, not picnickers. But we are pilgrims progressing somewhere, not merely hopeful travelers in search of a destination. The resurrection of Christ assures us that the promises of God are true and that we can count on them. In the midst of the deepest reality gap, we are following in the foot-steps of our Savior, and one day the gap will be closed, faith will be sight, and we will be forever with the Lord in glory. In the meantime, we say with joy, "The Lord is risen! He is risen indeed!"

FOR FURTHER REFLECTION

1. What did God promise Abram in Genesis 12?
2. How did a famine seem to jeopardize the fulfill-ment of all that God had promised?
3. How did Abram's sin jeopardize the fulfillment of all that God had promised?
4. In what ways do we find Abram to be like Christ in this passage? In what ways is he not at all like Christ?
5. Have you ever embarked on a mission for God, only to have everything go wrong right away? What did you learn through that experience?
6. Did Abram have the power to destroy God's pur-pose for his life by being disobedient? Or did even his sin serve to advance God's plan? Is the same thing true of our disobedience?
7. Egypt was a constant source of temptation to Abram, and later to Israel, whenever they doubted God's goodness or ability to keep his promises. To what do you turn when things go wrong and you doubt God's love and power?

3

TAKE THE MONEY
OR OPEN THE BOX
(GENESIS 13)

Iremember, when I was growing up, watching a TV game show in which contestants had to make the tough decision to "take the money or open the box." They could settle for the money they had already won or exchange everything for a mystery prize concealed in a box. That prize might be of much greater value than their winnings, such as a new car, the holiday of a lifetime, or a beautiful set of furniture. On the other hand, it might turn out to be something utterly worthless, such as a safety pin or a plastic garden gnome. What a difficult choice to have to make!

Many people think that having faith in God is just like that game show: we are being asked to stake everything on a massive leap in the dark, hoping against hope that there is a God out there who will catch us. One skeptic defined faith as "belief without evidence in what is told by one who speaks without knowledge, of things without parallel."[1] Or, as Mark Twain put it in his own inimitable style, "Faith is believing what you know ain't so."

Abram's faith, however, was not of that sort. His faith was not a blind faith. If it had been, he would have despaired when he saw the enormity of the difficulties that stood between him and the things promised by God. His continued trust in the midst of the reality gap shows us a man who knew that his future was controlled, not by an impartial game show host, but by a loving heavenly Father. The content of God's revelation to Abram was slim. It consisted of a brief oracle, promising that the Lord would turn him into the embodiment of blessing, plus whatever had been handed down to him of God's ancient dealings with his ancestors, generations before. It was not much, but that's what it means to live by faith. God reveals himself to us, and we respond to him trustingly, taking him at his word.

FAITH DEALING WITH FAILURE

We've already seen how Abram was propelled by the promises of God from a comfortable retirement to an unknown land, and how his faith faltered when he was put to the test of famine. Now, in this chapter, we will see—not for the last time—faith dealing with that failure. That's a very important lesson for us to learn, isn't it? There seem to be plenty of books telling you how to be a success, but few write about what to do when you find that you aren't. Yet what you do when you are at your lowest ebb, when everything has gone wrong and you have failed God and your neighbor utterly, says a great deal about the kind of person you are and the kind of faith you have. "Leap in the dark" faith cannot deal with personal failure, but real faith in the loving heavenly Father can provide the resources to survive it.

GOING BACK TO SQUARE ONE

How did Abram deal with his failure? He went back to square one. The opening verses of Genesis 13 show

Abram systematically reversing his tracks. He went back to the Negev (v. 1), where he was when he made the wrong decision to go down to Egypt (12:9). From there, he made a pilgrimage to Bethel (v. 3), to the place where he had pitched his tent earlier and where he had built an altar (12:8). There he called on the name of the Lord, just as he had on an earlier occasion (13:4; 12:8).

What kind of faith do you have? Does failure drive you away from God, or does it drive you back to square one, back to where you started, back to the altar, the place of sacrifice, so that you can call on the name of the Lord? The builders of the Tower of Babel made no room for offering sacrifices to God and calling on the name of the Lord. Their motto was "In man we trust." For that reason, when their building project fell apart, so did they. They had no means of dealing with failure. There was no room in their hearts for repentance, and consequently their religiosity could not survive the exposure of their own inadequacy. When the Lord judged them, they were scattered. But in Abram's case, failure was followed by repentance and a return to God. And so it is with all who have true faith. As the psalmist put it: "If the LORD delights in a man's way, he makes his steps firm; though he stumble, he will not fall, for the LORD upholds him with his hand" (Ps. 37:23).

Good people, people of faith, fail just as others do. The difference is that when they *fail,* they do not *fall,* because they return to the Lord in repentance, calling on his name and seeking forgiveness.

THE TEST OF PROSPERITY

Next, however, Abram was put to a new test, the test of prosperity. He and Lot were so blessed by God, and their herds and flocks increased so much, that they faced another crisis. Their possessions were so great that they were unable to stay together. Quarreling broke out among their herdsmen. We don't usually think of prosperity as being a testing condition. In fact, we usually think that if we just had a little more money, then many of our problems would be solved. This is a test that many of us would happily volunteer to undergo! How foolish we are! How little we recognize the dangers and risks that wealth brings in its wake! The apostle Paul knew its dangers better than we do. He wrote,

> I know what it is to be in need, and I know what it is to have plenty. I have learned the secret of being content in any and every situation, whether well fed or hungry, whether living in plenty or in want. I can do all things through him who gives me strength. (Phil. 4:12–13)

Paul had learned to be content in both conditions, whether well fed or hungry, rich or poor. Don't most of us think it difficult to be content only when poor? We would be quite happy to try being rich for a while. But if we are ever given the opportunity, we discover that riches solve few problems and can easily become a major obstacle to our spiritual growth. Think about it: If you won twenty-five million dollars, would that change your relationship to God? Would you still be dependent upon him for your daily bread? Would you still be faithful to the calling you have received from him? You *could* do a great deal of good with that much money. But there would be a great temptation to spend most or all of it on your own comfort. It would be hard not to say what the rich fool said to himself in the parable of Jesus: "You have plenty of good things laid up for many years. Take life easy; eat, drink and be merry" (Luke 12:19). I'm not sure I could handle that kind of "blessing." I think I would be better to stick to the prayer of Proverbs 30:8–9.

Give me neither poverty nor riches,
but give me only my daily bread.
Otherwise, I may have too much and disown
you
and say, "Who is the LORD?"
Or I may become poor and steal,
and so dishonor the name of my God.

In Abram's case, prosperity brought with it a real test of character. How would he handle the quarreling that had arisen? In some ways, the problem had a very simple solution. He was the senior partner with Lot, who was only his nephew. He could have simply sent Lot away to fend for himself, to make his own way in the world. No one would have criticized him for that. But Abram was not interested in grabbing the best land for himself. No, his faith in God led him to an act of almost incredible generosity. He allowed Lot to choose first. Because his eyes were firmly fixed on the promise of a heavenly inheritance, he could afford to renounce earthly desires. Indeed, a good measure of the health of your faith is your ability to give sacrificially.

At this point, a word of confession is in order. My wife, Barb, is much better at sacrificial giving than I am. I come from a long line of canny Scots who liked to know where every penny was at any given moment. Every purchase was the result of carefully deliberating the pros and cons. So giving freely to the Lord's work, even to the point of pain, didn't come naturally to me. It still doesn't. My wife, on the other hand, came from a missionary family that was used to not knowing precisely where the next paycheck was coming from, but was also used to it turning up nonetheless, sometimes from unexpected sources. That bred a level of dependence upon God from which I am still learning. But as my faith grows, along with it grows my ability to be truly generous with what the Lord has given us. As it says in the book of Proverbs, "He who is kind to the poor lends to the LORD, and he will reward him for what he has done" (Prov. 19:17).

LOT'S CHOICE

So it was that Lot made the first choice. But how did he choose? By sight. He chose the area that was "like the garden of the LORD, like the land of Egypt, toward Zoar" (Gen. 13:10). This superficially delightful description carries with it ominous undertones. Comparing it with "the garden of the LORD" is at least ambivalent. This depiction conjures up an image not only of fertility, but also of temptation and falling into sin. It also reminds us of the attempt of the builders of the Tower of Babel to take heaven by storm, without reference to God (11:4). Like them, Lot wanted to get around the cherubim guarding the way back to God's presence (3:24) and to enjoy the benefits of a place like that garden, without the inconvenience of having to please the Lord of the garden.

That has always been the way of materialism, which is quite eager to reach heaven, but has no interest in heaven's God. This mentality is quite prevalent in our contemporary world, where most people hope to go to heaven when they die. This is not surprising, given the generally acknowledged alternatives (either hell or nothingness). However, it is quite revealing to ask people what they hope to do when they get to heaven. Most people anticipate the joys of this world writ large: golf courses with no sand traps or water hazards, heavenly mansions with no worries about mortgage payments. If they could have all of those things without leaving this planet, they would be more than content. Christians, however, long for heaven because they long to be in the nearer presence of the God whom they love with all their hearts, joining in the unstinted, eternal worship of the

Lamb. As the Puritan Richard Baxter perceptively commented centuries ago,

> There is a great deal of difference between the desires of heaven in a sanctified man and an unsanctified. The believer prizeth it above earth, and had rather be with God than here . . . but to the ungodly there is nothing seemeth more desirable than this world; and therefore he only chooseth heaven before hell, but not before earth.[2]

Describing the land chosen by Lot as "like the land of Egypt" further reinforces the image of dangerous prosperity. Egypt was the place of compromise from which God had just delivered Abram and Lot. Already it appears that Lot would have been quite happy to stay there, outside the land of blessing. The importance of this is underlined by the fact that the original readers of this account in the time of Moses had just emerged from captivity in Egypt, and its continuing attraction was all too real to them, also.

Genesis 13:10 adds parenthetically, "This was before the LORD destroyed Sodom and Gomorrah." This emphasizes the hidden dangers of Lot's choice even more. In choosing with his eyes, Lot entrusted his life to a dangerously flawed sense. It didn't seem to matter to Lot that the land that he was choosing was only on the edge of the Promised Land, if not actually outside it. His "faith" did not seem to affect this crucial decision of his life.

Once he was on this path of compromise, he progressed comfortably and easily along it. Lot started out living *"near* Sodom" (13:12). Soon he was living *"in* Sodom" (14:12). Then he was "sitting in the gateway of the city" (19:1), which suggests that he held a position of respect among the citizens of Sodom, and his daughters were pledged to marry inhabitants of the city (19:14). It is the old story of the frog in the kettle. Put a frog into a kettle of boiling water, and he will immediately leap out; put him into a pan of cold water and heat it slowly, and he will stay there until he is nicely cooked.

The way of the world often seems to offer greener grass than God's way. Satan's shortcuts always give the impression of saving effort and hardship. If your choices in life are determined by whatever appeals to your eyes, then Satan will make short work of you. All he has to do is hide his hook in a juicy enough worm and you'll swallow it hook, line, and sinker. How do you resist Satan's tempting alternatives? Often in life we get hooked because we try to nibble the worm "just a little." We want to see how close we can get to the hook without getting caught. We want to dance around the margins of sin without getting sucked in. The trouble is that, as Lot found, one thing so easily leads to another. Like a whirlpool, sin has a powerful vortex effect. Before we know it, we find ourselves in over our heads—and getting out is so much harder than getting in.

The problem is exacerbated by Satan's skill as a debater. He easily persuaded Lot that he could live next to the inhabitants of Sodom and Gomorrah without risk. He could as easily persuade you that you will not suffer the consequences of your sin. "Go ahead, have that affair. You'll never get caught," he whispers. "No one will ever discover your hypocrisy." How many people discover to their great loss, as Lot did, that Satan has been a liar from the beginning? His constant goal is to get believers to turn their backs on the promises of God and pursue apparently rosier dreams.

How then can we answer Satan's subtleties? How can we train ourselves to look past the worm and see the hook? The answer is to fix our eyes on our heavenly inheritance, on God himself. In the movie *Chariots of Fire*, there is a moment when the Scottish athlete Eric Liddell defends his focus on running by telling his sister, "When I run, I feel God's pleasure." It was that same all-consuming desire to "feel God's pleasure" that caused him to refuse to run in the Olympic heats when they were scheduled on a Sunday. Despite immense pressure from the British team officials and the Prince of Wales himself, Liddell steadfastly refused to compromise, because he sought the approval of a higher authority. You and I need to learn how to live lives that are motivated by the same desire to please God, to "feel God's pleasure," no matter what those around us think. Like Joseph, when he was tempted by Potiphar's wife, we need to see that behind the attractive front of whatever Satan is offering us lies the hook: sin against the God for whom we live. In spite of all his subtlety, Satan has yet to develop a convincing response to the saint who cries out, "How then could I do such a wicked thing and sin against God?" (Gen. 39:9).

ABRAM'S CHOICE

In contrast to Lot's compromising materialism, Abram's faith was rewarded with a renewed promise. The one who refused to live by sight was now told to lift up his eyes and look in all directions. All the land that he could see was to be his, and his offspring were to be as numerous as the dust of the earth (Gen. 13:14–16). The terms of the Lord's promise to Abram in Genesis 12:7 had now been expanded. God invited him to walk throughout the land, to see the goodness of the gift that God would give. Yet he never did receive the full ownership of that property here on earth. Like Moses after him, Abram looked to an inheritance ultimately beyond this world. As the apostle Paul puts it, "If only for this life we have hope in Christ, we are to be pitied more than all men" (1 Cor. 15:19). Abram's hope had to be in something more substantial than a nice piece of property, some prime real estate with a white picket fence around it. It was an eternal hope. He was looking for a city with foundations, which God himself would build (Heb. 11:10). But how could that be? How could Abram, the failure, be accepted by God? He could be accepted only by faith, which casts itself upon the promise of God and rests there securely.

The ultimate answer to how Abram could be accepted in spite of his failure came much later, in another encounter with Satan. On that occasion, the Devil took Jesus up onto a very high mountain and showed him all the kingdoms of the world and their splendor, and promised to give them all to Jesus if he would just bow down and worship him (Matt. 4:8–9). Satan was offering Jesus the Promised Land without the cross. All the kingdoms of the earth were on the table, and Jesus walked away. Why? They were his by rights! Why shouldn't he claim them then and there? Because Jesus knew that Satan was offering the kingdoms of the earth apart from the plan of God, which meant possessing them without saving God's people. Jesus' love for the Father and for us was such that he would follow the path of suffering so that he could redeem us, rather than possess the whole world without us. For our sake, he chose the pain-filled way of the Father's pleasure.

Lot opted to "take the money." He chose with his eyes and took the apparently easy prosperity that was offered to him. It was a decision he would live to regret. Turning his back on the Land of Promise meant turning his back on the pathway to blessing. By contrast, Abram trusted God and "opened the box." There were no guarantees of worldly prosperity or security. There was simply God's promise to be his God now and forever, a promise that would ultimately take Christ all the way to the cross. That promise was enough for Abram; it should be more than enough for you and me.

FOR FURTHER REFLECTION

1. Where did Abram go after leaving Egypt? What do Abram's actions say about his attitude toward God?

2. How did Abram's offer and Lot's choice reveal their attitudes toward wealth?
3. How did Abram set us a good example of how to deal with spiritual failure? How was his response different from that of Adam and Eve after they disobeyed in the Garden of Eden?
4. How did Lot make his decision, and what sins tempt us today in the same way? What practical measures could you take in your life to decrease the power of these sins?
5. God gradually revealed his great plan to Abram, bit by bit. How was Abram's experience of God so far like yours or different from yours?
6. How did Abram go about determining God's will? What two helps do we have today that he did not have, and how does that change the process of finding God's will for us?

4

IN THE DAYS OF
GOOD KING ABRAM
(GENESIS 14)

Give me one moment in time
When I'm more than I thought I could be,
When all of my dreams are a heartbeat away,
And the answers are all up to me.[1]

So sang Whitney Houston as the theme song of the 1992 Olympic Games, held in Barcelona. It exactly captured the Olympic ideal. That is what the athletes seek for and get—if they are fortunate. There is that one brief moment in the public eye, when their dreams are put to the test, before they sink back into relative obscurity. In this brief moment of glory, the truth is told about their ability to perform at the highest level.

Abram, too, had "one moment in time," and it is recorded in the fourteenth chapter of Genesis. He was prosperous, but he was still only a wandering nomad, like so many others around him. There was nothing obvious that marked him out as the divinely appointed heir to the land of Canaan. To the casual observer, he must have looked very ordinary. In this chapter, however, the veil is lifted for a moment, and we see Abram in his true colors, acting as the king of the land that is his by right and that will be inherited by his offspring. This is Abram's mount of transfiguration, when his glory is clearly—if briefly—revealed to those closest to him.

A CLASSIC MILITARY CAMPAIGN

Genesis 14 opens with an account of a classic ancient military campaign. Verses 1–11 could have been drawn from the annals of any great king in the ancient Near East. The cycle of the subjection of a people, followed by their rebellion, followed by the great king's crushing defeat of his enemies and their resubjection to him, was a common one. In an age when might made right, the authority of an overlord was frequently put to the test. If the overlord managed to retain his power, his victory would be recorded in his annals in glowing terms, no doubt as a deterrent to others of a similar mind. Such is the kind of conflict recorded for us in the early verses of Genesis 14: the struggle between the forces of a great king and his allies, on the one hand, and his rebellious subject peoples, on the other.

In that struggle, Lot was caught up almost by accident—almost, but not entirely! For it was not completely by coincidence that he happened to be residing in Sodom. He may have considered himself an uninvolved bystander, but he was there in pursuit of his own material gain. He had chosen the land that was like the Garden of Eden (Gen. 13:10), only to discover later the snake in the grass—Sodom. After turning his back on the Promised Land and on Abram, Lot experienced a period of decline, during which only Abram's repeated interventions rescued him from total destruction (Gen. 14–19).

At issue was a broader theological question: Will a righteous man who dwells in the midst of the wicked get caught up in their destruction? Will the Lord sweep away the righteous with the wicked? The question is not formally put to God by Abram until Genesis 18:23, but it constitutes the background to this part of Lot's story as well. According to Peter, the experience of Lot teaches us that "the Lord knows how to rescue godly men from trials and to hold the unrighteous for the day of judgment, while continuing their punishment" (2 Peter 2:9).

This truth is a comfort to all of us who must live in the real world of difficult decisions and hard choices, where we are frequently forced into the company of those whose language, lifestyle, and behavior make us wince. Yet Lot's story also provides a challenge to those of us who live too comfortably alongside those who are of an entirely different spirit from us. Many of us, like Lot, have happily settled down in this world and assimilated ourselves to our environment. We need to remember that it isn't easy to live in a pigsty without ending up smelling like a pig. While God can easily rescue the godly from the judgment that is to come on the wicked, it is not nearly as easy as we think to remain godly while living in the close company of the wicked. Although God delivered Lot from the judgment he brought on Sodom, Lot hardly emerged unscathed, as we shall see.

A THREAT TO THE PROMISE

There was also another dimension to the kidnapping of Lot. It was not simply something that happened to a righteous person who happened to be living a somewhat compromised lifestyle. Rather, it was a threat to the promise of descendants and land that God had given to Abram. After all, at this point in the story, Lot was the only family that Abram had. What good is a Promised Land if at any moment a mighty army of foreigners can sweep across it and carry you off into exile? Could the

Lord protect Abram's family and land from the perennial danger of foreign assaults?

The Lord could indeed, and he would. His chosen instrument to accomplish all of this was Abram. Abram could easily have left Lot to his fate. Remember that Lot had selfishly chosen what looked like the best portion of the land, had foolishly linked his fortunes with notoriously wicked people, and, in the process, had distanced himself from his best and truest friend. In other words, in sharing the fate of Sodom, Lot was simply getting what was coming to him as the natural result of his sinful choices. Moreover, in pursuing him, Abram was taking a considerable personal risk. The force that carried Lot off may have been a small, fast-moving raiding party, rather than a huge army, but they were undoubtedly backed by the significant resources of a major alliance. That is why the opening verses of the chapter are written in the style of the annals of a great king. Indeed, the lead king in the alliance was none other than Amraphel, king of Shinar (14:1), that is, king of Babylon (cf. Gen. 10:10; 11:2, 9). By rescuing Lot, Abram was making some powerful enemies, and his own forces were pitifully small. But Abram, the man of faith, knew the principle put into words many years later: "Nothing can hinder the LORD from saving, whether by many or by few" (1 Sam. 14:6).

Here too there is a challenge to each of us. When assessing whether or not to intervene in a situation, we typically base our decision on the answers to two questions. First, does this person deserve my help? Second, can I help him without any risk or inconvenience to myself? If the answer to both of these questions is yes, we are normally glad to do what we can for the other person. However, if the answer to either or both questions is no, we tend to hold back. In our ministry to the poor, for example, we look for "deserving" poor people to help—those who are poor through no evident fault of their own. In addition, we look for "clean" ministries by which we can help them. We will send money to a charity that works with such people, or go on a two-week mission trip to the Third World or the inner city, while ignoring the messy task of ministering to the homeless in our own community.

HIS BROTHER'S KEEPER

But Abram did not think in such terms. Lot did not deserve to be rescued. He had gotten himself into this mess. Nor was helping him risk free. Abram was staking his life on a highly dangerous venture. But the bottom line was that Lot was his kinsman, literally (in the Hebrew) "his brother" (Gen. 14:14), and he needed Abram's assistance. And so Abram took up his sword and set out to rescue him. He would not fight to assert his right to own the land, even though the Lord had given it to him. But, as the divinely appointed ruler of the land, he would use the sword to intervene on behalf of his oppressed subjects, even though they did not recognize his sovereignty over them. He overtook the forces of the four mighty kings at the northern border of the Promised Land, at Dan. There he won a resounding victory, rescued Lot, and returned with all the spoil that had been plundered from Sodom.

In all of this, do we not see a picture of Jesus Christ? He did not sit idly in heaven, waiting for us to deserve to be redeemed. If he had, eternity would have gone by without our redemption. Nor was our redemption risk free and painless. Christ was willing to leave the glories of heaven and come down to us, taking the form of a servant in our midst. When necessary, as king of his people, he took up a whip to clear the hucksters and merchants out of the temple (Matt. 21:12–13). As king of the Jews, he intervened powerfully to assure justice for his oppressed people. Yet in his own hour of need, he told his disciples to put away their swords, and he refused to call the angelic hosts to his defense (Matt. 26:52–54). His own people, however, rejected him, nailing him to the cross, ironically beneath a sign that read "The king of the Jews." Jesus was willing not only to take risks for the sake of his undeserving kinsmen, but also to suffer great agony for them on the cross. But there on the cross, as in the person of Melchizedek, righteousness and peace met. There we find not only the proof that Jesus loves us, but also the pain-filled means by which he powerfully delivered the undeserving people he had chosen for himself, even in the face of their estrangement and ingratitude toward him. How great is the love that God has shown us! As the apostle Paul reminds us, "God demonstrates his own love for us in this: While we were still sinners, Christ died for us" (Rom. 5:8).

How then shall we, who are called by his name, refuse to help others on the grounds that they are undeserving, or that helping them might endanger our comfort and security? If we are truly his disciples, we will be like the Good Samaritan, who resolved to help first and ask questions later. To be sure, sometimes truly helping someone demands tough love, matching assistance with signs of repentance. Sometimes we must refuse to give a handout that would simply allow someone to remain enslaved in sinful habits. But our criterion for refusing to give assistance can only be whether our action can genuinely help the person, not whether he deserves the help or whether we will be inconvenienced.

A SECOND CONFLICT

On his return, Abram was faced with another struggle, a much more subtle one. It came in the approach of the two kings, Melchizedek, king of Salem, and the unnamed king of Sodom. These two kings are a study in contrasts. Melchizedek's very name means "king of righteousness," and the name of his city means "peace"; the king of Sodom, on the other hand, ruled over a territory that has become a byword in the language of abominations. Melchizedek came as the priest of God Most High and offered to Abram the priestly elements of life, bread, and wine, pronouncing a gracious blessing upon Abram and praising God for Abram's victory. By contrast, the king of Sodom came with words that were gruff and grudging. He offered no thanks to Abram for being rescued and did not acknowledge God's role in the victory. He simply approached Abram with a business offer: "Let's make a deal; I'll keep the people, you get the goods." He regarded it as a simple human victory, with the normal human consequences.

The final contrast between the two kings came in the working out of the principle of Genesis 12:3, "I will bless those who bless you, and whoever curses you I will curse." Melchizedek came graciously to Abram and received a blessing from him, a tithe of everything he had captured. The king of Sodom, however, simply hammered another nail into the coffin whose lid would soon slam shut (Gen. 19).

Which of these two contrasting approaches did Abram choose to follow? The drawbacks in the king of Sodom's offer would have been evident only to the eye of faith. Superficially, it must have seemed attractive to Abram to take credit for the victory, and therefore to keep all the proceeds. Would Abram choose the way of humble obedience and devotion to God Most High, represented by Melchizedek, or the earthly "get rich quick" scheme of the king of Sodom?

Abram took the way of faith. Faith would rather eat a basic diet of life's staples in the company of the righteous than feast in the company of the wicked. Abram recognized that the victory was God's by offering to his representative a tenth of all the spoils. The rest—apart from the rightful share of his allies—he returned to the king of Sodom. Faith chooses to receive God's blessing—intangible as that may be—rather than be rewarded materially by the wicked. Unlike Lot, Abram was still committed to the way of separateness. He trusted God to deliver in his own time and in his own way the riches of the promise.

Yet Abram must have been tempted to take matters into his own hands. It must have seemed attractive to take a shortcut and seize what God had promised. The Promised Land now lay at his feet. It looked as if he could seize a large part of it and possess both people and land. Satan must have been whispering to him, as he would later to Jesus, "All this will I give you, if you will bow down and worship me" (Matt. 4:9). Here was a test every bit as searching of his faith as when an escapee came to him earlier, desperately seeking help (14:13). Then he had to draw his sword, against all human wisdom, to rescue his undeserving relative. Now he had to sheath his sword, once again against all human wisdom, to wait for God's time to inherit the land. God's time to give him the land had not yet come, and Abram would rather wait for God's time—even if he might die waiting—than stretch out his hand to snatch the forbidden fruit. In his patient faith, Abram provided a graphic contrast to Adam and Eve, who were so easily convinced to doubt God's word and to believe the Serpent's lies.

What about us? Satan still loves to offer plausible shortcuts that seem to bring us good ends by an easier way. Here are some of the areas in which he may offer you a shortcut:

- *Sexuality:* Why wait for marriage? If sex is a good gift from God, and two people are really in love, why does it have to be confined within such rigid boundaries?
- *Business ethics:* Everybody else arrives late and takes off early; everyone else cheats on taxes and

finesses the expense account. So why shouldn't I? Why should I miss out on such an easy gain? Neither the company nor the government will really miss it.

- *Giving:* How much should I give to the church? Isn't 10 percent a bit legalistic? Let's be realistic about what I can afford. After all, the cost of living is high these days.

And so it goes on. The temptation is always there to think that we can shave a few corners and take a few shortcuts without missing out on God's blessing. Abram recognized where that kind of logic led, and he would have none of it.

MELCHIZEDEK AND JESUS

But in this same chapter, where we see Abram portrayed at his most ideal, as the man of faith acting as king of the land that was his by right, we see also the mysterious figure of Melchizedek towering over him. Although there is great blessing to be found in Abram, here is one who is even greater than Abram. In the New Testament, the book of Hebrews picks up this idea and points out how Melchizedek prefigures Christ, especially in his priesthood. The writer to the Hebrews gives us three points of comparison between Melchizedek and Jesus.

- *His was a priesthood established not on the basis of heredity but office.* In other words, Melchizedek was a priest not simply because his father had been one, but because he was king of Salem. It was all part of his job description. Similarly, Jesus was not a priest because of heredity—he did not come from the priestly tribe of Levi—but because he was the Messiah, the King, the Son of David. In that sense, Jesus was a priest after the order of Melchizedek (Heb. 6:20).

- *His was an eternal priesthood.* There is no mention of Melchizedek having any successor. His priestly office, as far as the Bible is concerned, was fulfilled in this one man. For the Levitical priesthood, however, there was a great deal of concern to ensure a proper succession. Sacrifices had to be offered continually, and Levitical priests had the habit of dying like other people. But this was not true of Jesus. He needed no successors because his sacrifice was offered once and for all. Furthermore, having been raised from the dead, he has been able to intercede for his people perpetually.

- *His was a superior priesthood.* Abram submitted himself to Melchizedek and gave him a tithe. This was particularly striking, since elsewhere Abram acted as the priest for his own family. Normally he built his own altars and offered his own sacrifices. But here he is, recognizing the priesthood of another. In a sense, then, Levi, though yet unborn, submitted to Melchizedek in the person of his ancestor and so recognized the superiority of his priesthood. Thus, Jesus, the priest after the order of Melchizedek, holds a priesthood that is superior to the Levitical priesthood.

But why do we need a superior priesthood? The reason is that the Old Testament priesthood could never really deal with sin. The blood of assorted animals was never enough and could never have been enough to pay for our rebellion against an infinitely holy and majestic God. The prophet Micah sensed this when he wrote,

With what shall I come before the LORD and bow down before the exalted God? Shall I come before him with burnt offerings, with calves a year old? Will the Lord be pleased with thousands of rams, with ten thousand rivers of oil? Shall I offer my firstborn for my transgression, the fruit of my body for the sin of my soul? (Micah 6:6–7)

None of this could ever be enough. But the blood of Jesus can deal with sin and save us completely. On the cross, Jesus died, once and for all, the righteous in the place of the unrighteous, the perfect Son of God in the place of sinful creatures. And now, having been raised from the dead, he lives forever to intercede on our behalf. In Jesus we find the effective priest that we need.

Thus, Abram recognizes, even in his "one moment in time," that here is another, greater than he, through whom he must approach God Most High. In Melchizedek he recognizes a forerunner of the great High Priest to come, Jesus Christ, who would offer the perfect sacrifice once and for all for him. Abram recognized that greatness in God's kingdom is not simply a matter of doing mighty deeds for God and rescuing the undeserving. It also involves coming to God through the priest that God has established.

Like Abram, we need Jesus, not only in our hour of failure, but also in our hour of greatest triumph. We need to run to the cross, not only when we have sinned against God and man, but also when we have faced our greatest temptation victoriously. For Jesus is our great High Priest, whose sacrifice paid not only for our sins, but also for our righteousness, which even at its best is still woefully inadequate. There on the cross he replaced both with his perfect righteousness, the only garment in which we may stand in the presence of the all-holy God, our Creator and Redeemer. Even at our best, doing our best can never be sufficient to earn a place in heaven. Only as we stand in Jesus may we feel the pleasure of God Most High upon us, his unworthy servants.

FOR FURTHER REFLECTION

1. How did Lot's behavior and predicament jeopardize the fulfillment of God's promises to Abram? Did Lot deserve Abram's help?
2. How did Abram's response to the two kings fulfill God's initial promise to Abram in Genesis 12:2–4?
3. Look up Hebrews 6:20–7:19. How was Melchizedek like Jesus? Why did Abram give him a tithe and honor his priesthood?
4. Lot shared the fate of the Sodomites because he lived close to them. How are you affected by the choices you make concerning friends, workplace, church, and living arrangements?
5. Abram didn't seize this opportunity to grasp the Promised Land, but waited for God to give it to him. What promises are we waiting for, and how are we tempted to grasp what God has promised by taking shortcuts instead of waiting for God?
6. Abram rejected the plunder offered by the king of Sodom because he refused to be made rich by anyone except God. How does God make us rich? How are our riches a testimony to the world that we belong to God?

5

FAITH LAYING HOLD
OF GOD
(GENESIS 15)

Satan's prime strategy is to tempt us to doubt God's goodness. It has worked well for him in the past. It was the strategy with which he deceived Eve in the Garden of Eden: "Did God really say . . . ?" Is God really looking out for your best interests? If the planting of doubt worked so well in the Garden, how much more effective will it be in our fallen world, where a gap exists between God's promises and much of our experience! So we find ourselves asking, "Is this problem I'm facing right now ever really going to be resolved? What if, far from the situation resolving itself, such and such happens? What will become of me then?"

Often that temptation comes in its strongest form right after we've hit the heights, immediately after our "one moment in time." Think of the experience of the prophet Elijah. One day he was on the mountaintop, exposing the prophets of Baal as frauds and demonstrating that the Lord is the only true God (1 Kings 18). The next thing you know, however, he was alarmed by a death threat from Queen Jezebel. In no time, he was running for his life, depressed enough to pray that he might die (1

Kings 19:4). Satan was whispering to him, "Is this God whom you serve really good? Is this any way to reward his loyal servants?"

DOUBTING THE PROMISE

After Abram rescued Lot and overcame the temptation to grasp the Promised Land in his own strength (Gen. 15), the word of the Lord came to him once again, reiterating the promise: "Do not be afraid, Abram. I am your shield, your very great reward" (16:1). But, in practical terms, the promise seemed as far away from fulfillment as ever. Lot had apparently gone back to Sodom, and now someone who was not even a relative of Abram's stood to inherit his estate. In spite of his faithful obedience to God, Abram still had neither offspring nor ownership of the smallest portion of the Land of Promise. For Abram, as for Moses' original audience in the wilderness, there was no visible evidence to support his faith. The reality gap appeared to be as wide as ever, a situation in which the temptation to second-guess the decision to be faithful to God was strong.

Abram was discovering that God's promises continually demand faith from us to bridge the reality gap. But what are you to do when you feel you don't have enough faith? What are you to do when you fear that your grasp on God's promises is slipping? Abram began to fear that he would never see his promised posterity, and that his present earthly portion would be all that he would ever receive from God. Now many people would have been satisfied with that. Life had been good to Abram. Materially, he had prospered greatly. But Abram was not content with the good life. He hungered to see God's purpose and promises fulfilled.

I find Abram's hunger to see God's promises become a reality very challenging. What are your goals for the next year, or the next five years? Will you be content simply to say, "Life has been good"? Will you be satisfied simply to prosper materially? Or do you hunger and thirst after righteousness? Do you burn to see God's kingdom advancing in and through you? That is what is at issue here. Abram was not simply looking for an heir to whom he could leave what he had accumulated. Eliezer of Damascus would have served that purpose. Nor was he simply in love with babies, in search of a cuddly Abram Junior with a heart-melting smile. He wanted to see God's purpose of blessing the whole world through him carried out. Is it too much to say that he was looking for the promised seed of Genesis 3:15, the one who would come and crush the Serpent's head once and for all? From where would this promised Savior come? How would God fulfill his promises?

LAYING OUT DOUBTS

So what *should* you do when the reality gap overwhelms your faith? You should lay it all out before God. Abram opened all his concerns out before God. Even doubting thoughts and feelings that border on sin are better laid out before the gracious eyes of the Lord than nursed in our hearts. God will not be shocked! He knows our inmost thoughts anyway!

And Abram was not sent away empty-handed. The word of the Lord came to him again. Here we see Abram the prophet (as Genesis 20:7 calls him). He once again received a direct message from God. He received a renewed promise of a son and of descendants like the stars. What is more, as he responded in faith to God's calling, the promise was gradually becoming more detailed. His heir would not be a servant, nor even a distant relative like Lot, but rather a son from his own body. This is often true in the lives of Christians today. The further you go in obedience, the more you see of God's plan. God doesn't often tell us the end from the beginning. He prefers to lead us on step-by-step in dependence upon him.

It was most appropriate for God to take Abram outside and tell him to gaze up into the night sky. The one who called the stars into existence out of nothing could surely also raise up a son for one who was beyond all human hope and help. As the prophet Jeremiah put it: "Ah, Sovereign LORD, you have made the heavens and the earth by your great power and outstretched arm. Nothing is too hard for you" (Jer. 32:17).

BELIEVING GOD

"Abram believed the LORD" (Gen. 15:6a). These simple words hide a profound reality. Abram's faith laid hold of God, "and he credited it to him as righteousness" (v. 6b). The form of the Hebrew verb translated "believed" points to this being a repeated or continuous action. Faith was Abram's normal response to God's words. His attitude of trust was that summed up in the words of a bumper sticker: "God said it; I believe it; that settles it." There is no special power that resides in an attitude of trust. Abram's faith was not in the power of faith itself. Nor was it a leap in the dark. Abram's faith was a settled conviction that God would do what he had promised, no matter what. It was such faith alone that justified Abram.

Abram didn't go out and immediately perform a mighty deed for God as a result of his faith. He simply believed in the free promise of God and took him at his word. It was that attitude of faith that was reckoned to him as righteousness.

The righteous man in the Old Testament is the one whom God will save because he is in a right relationship with God. Normally the word *righteous* reflects moral actions: the righteous person lives a moral life. In Psalm 15:2–5, for example, the righteous person is the one

> who speaks the truth from his heart
> > and has no slander on his tongue,
> who does his neighbor no wrong
> > and casts no slur on his fellow man,
> who despises a vile man
> > but honors those who fear the LORD,
> who keeps his oath
> > even when it hurts,
> who lends his money without usury
> > and does not accept a bribe against the inno-
> > > cent.

But here in Genesis 15, it is Abram's simple faith that is reckoned to him as righteousness. Certainly his faith led him to perform good works—otherwise it could hardly be called faith at all. But at the moment in which Abram was justified before God, faith was all alone. As the hymn writers put it,

> Nothing in my hand I bring; simply to thy cross
> > I cling.[1]

> Just as I am, without one plea, save that thy
> > blood was shed for me.[2]

Faith does not look at itself at all. It looks entirely to God and finds in him a righteousness that is not our own, but is reckoned to us.

It is faith that bridges the reality gap. The same apparent contradictions still confronted Abram. How could God do what he had promised? How could a man almost one hundred years old have a son? We too sometimes face such hard questions and apparent contradictions. How is it possible for God to be both perfectly holy and the one who justifies the ungodly? How could the sins of someone like me, who blows it over and over again, be forgiven? Is it possible that the church of Jesus Christ, with all its faults and failings, can survive and prosper in such a day as ours? Faith silences our questions and lays hold of the one who does the impossible.

GOD'S SIGN

Abram, believing God's promises, asked for a sign (v. 8). This was not the request of unbelief, but of faith. He desired a token by which God would give him assurance of his promises. What he received was something breathtakingly awesome. He received the covenant commitment of God (vv. 18–21), a commitment sealed by what seems to us today a very strange ceremony (vv. 9–17). Abram was told to prepare various sacrificial animals—a heifer, a goat, and a ram, along with a dove and a pigeon—by cutting them in half. If we saw Abram the king in the previous chapter and Abram the prophet earlier in this chapter, here we see Abram the priest getting all the necessary items ready for the covenant ceremony.

A covenant was a common form of agreement in the ancient Near East. There were several different kinds of covenants. Some covenants were made between big, powerful nations and their small, weak neighbors. The king of the powerful nation would offer the king of the smaller nation certain benefits, like protection against being attacked by other countries, and in return the weaker king would swear loyalty and obedience to the stronger king. Like a Mafia protection policy, it was usually an offer you couldn't safely refuse! Other covenants were made between a king and a loyal subject, who was granted a piece of land as a reward for faithful service. The covenant with Abram in Genesis 15 belongs in the latter category. So here in verse 7 the Lord proclaims: "I am the LORD, who brought you out of Ur of the Chaldeans to give you this land."

At the conclusion of a covenant agreement, it was sometimes the custom for the parties to walk between the pieces of a torn-up animal. This served as a kind of acted-out curse. What they were saying was, "If I break the covenant, may I be torn to pieces like this animal." But in God's covenant with Abram, only one of the parties passed between the pieces: God himself in the form of a blazing, smoking torch (v. 17). That foreshadowed the pillars of cloud and fire on Mount Sinai. The one who would give the law was here showing that grace comes first, for this was a totally one-sided covenant. It depended entirely on God for its fulfillment. Do you see how amazing this was? God, the ever-living One, was saying, "I would rather be torn apart than see my relationship with humanity broken, the relationship that I have promised to establish through Abram's descendant."

By what figure could God have demonstrated his commitment more graphically to Abram? How could it have been displayed more vividly? The only way would have been for the figure to become a reality, for the ever-living God to take on human nature and taste death in the place of the covenant-breaking children of Abram. And that is precisely what God did in Jesus Christ. On the cross, the covenant curse fell completely on Jesus, so that the guilty ones who place their trust in him might experience the blessings of the covenant. Jesus bore the punishment for our sins, so that God might be our God and we might be his people. Each time we celebrate the Lord's Supper, we proclaim God in human form, broken for us and for our transgressions, so that our relationship with him might be restored.

The sacrifices that Abram laid out were those of the Old Testament, of the Levitical order. They were the sacrifices that would be established on Sinai. Yet the blood of bulls and goats and birds cannot take away our sin. They point forward to the blood of the covenant, the blood of Jesus, poured out for us on the cross. Without the shedding of *that* blood, there could be no remission of our sins. In the words of the hymn writer Cecil Alexander,

> There was no other good enough to pay the
> price of sin,
> He only could unlock the gate of heav'n and let
> me in.[3]

A PROMISE DELAYED

Abram himself would not live to see that day. As he looked forward, he recognized, however dimly, that God would bring about the salvation of his people, but he was warned against any overly enthusiastic expectation of earthly blessing. The first installment, the Promised Land, would not be received for many years—and even then it would come after much difficulty. Exile would come first—exile in Egypt and four hundred years of mistreatment—before the Promised Land could finally be entered.

Abram was a true prophet: the events that the Lord revealed to him came to pass. First came the suffering; then came the glory. That order remains true for us as Christians. In Acts 14:22, Paul and Barnabas reminded those who had become Christians on their first missionary journey that this fundamental pattern hasn't changed: "We must go through many hardships to enter the kingdom of God."

As for Abram himself, his own departure would come peacefully after many days. What more could anyone ask? But God's promise would remain largely unfulfilled on this side of the grave. Abram had to realize that the land that he sought was a heavenly country, not an earthly one. God was good, very good, to Abram. But the chief and crowning blessing awaited him on the other side of the grave. It is ever so for believers: even when we experience the blessings of God in great measure here and now, the best is yet to come.

Why, though, was there such a delay in the fulfillment of the promise? Was God being slow in delivering what he had promised, like a parent regretting a word rashly spoken? By no means! But the fulfillment of the promise to Abram meant judgment on the occupants of the land, and the sin of the Amorites was not yet full (Gen. 15:16). This is why we continue to see the wicked prospering in our midst. God's forbearance is not yet exhausted. There is still time left for repentance—and who are we, as forgiven sinners, to wish it any other way? But God's patience with the wicked is not unlimited, as the residents of Sodom and Gomorrah would soon discover.

Abram believed God and it was reckoned to him as righteousness. Why? Not because he was perfect—the Scriptures are painfully honest in revealing his flaws and shortcomings. But it was reckoned to him as righteousness because his faith was in God, who would in Christ bear the covenant curse himself. His faith was in him who in Christ lived the perfect life on behalf of his people. So it is for all who will repent and believe during this period of forbearance before Jesus Christ returns to judge the world. There is forgiveness and new life for the one who takes hold of the covenant-keeping God by faith. As surely as Abram's descendants would possess the land that God had promised them, so shall his spiritual children possess the heavenly Land of Promise.

FOR FURTHER REFLECTION

1. How does God's promise to Abram in Genesis 15 differ from the two previous promises in Genesis 12:2–3 and 13:14–17?

2. How did God's sign (Gen. 15:8–21) answer Abram's doubt?
3. Why was the fulfillment of the promise delayed?
4. Abram doubted God, yet was not disobedient. What is the difference between obedient doubt and rebellious doubt?
5. How did the covenant ceremony recorded in chapter 15 foreshadow Christ? What is the significance of the fact that only God passed through the pieces?
6. How does this chapter of the Bible help you to deal with the reality gaps in your life?

6

FAITH STUMBLING

(GENESIS 16)

In the past three chapters, we've seen Abram at his very best: Abram the man of faith as prophet, priest, and king. Now, in Genesis 16, we are confronted again with Abram the failure. In one sense, this is a comforting image for us. The great man of faith was also a man tempted just as we are. Yet this is also a challenge to us. If such a great hero of the faith can be led astray so easily, so also can we. As Paul puts it, "If you think you are standing firm, be careful that you don't fall!" (1 Cor. 10:12).

The chapter opens with a restatement of Abram's ongoing problem: "Now Sarai, Abram's wife, had borne him no children." In spite of God's promise of numerous offspring, the nursery was still painfully empty. Often in the Bible, such a statement is followed by God's stepping in miraculously to remove the problem. But not here. Instead, Sarai thinks that she has the solution, in the person of her Egyptian maidservant, Hagar. What we have here is a classic human attempt to solve a problem with man's wisdom, not God's.

THE ANATOMY OF TEMPTATION

Like Adam before him, Abram found temptation approaching in the person of his nearest and dearest. We often forget that temptation can come from any quarter, even from within our own family circle. We expect the Devil to assault us like a roaring lion, as ugly and fearsome as can be. We don't expect him to come to us dressed up like an angel of light, speaking in the honey-sweet tones of the ones we love. Yet the Bible warns us that such an approach is easy for him to adopt (2 Cor. 11:14). Thus, Satan didn't only confront Jesus head-on in the wilderness (Matt. 4:1–11); he also tempted him more subtly through the words of one of his closest disciples, Peter (Matt. 16:23).

Like Adam, Abram capitulated readily to a temptation that might not have deceived him if it had come from a different source. The parallel between the two experiences is underlined in the original Hebrew by the use of the same idiom: Adam and Abram both "hearkened to the voice of" their wives (Gen. 3:17; 16:2). What is more, in both cases the woman "took" and "gave" to her husband (Gen. 3:6; 16:3). There was an inversion of the proper spiritual leadership structure in the home, and the result in each case was disaster. Of course, listening to your wife is not necessarily wrong! In Genesis 21:12, God specifically commands Abraham to listen to his wife because in this instance she is right. But we need to be aware that the very person intended to be a blessing to us may also be the one through whom we are led astray. The only protection is for us to be so thoroughly attuned to God's Word that we are able to recognize and resist temptation from whatever source it comes. Obedience must be more precious than even the closest of human relationships (Matt. 10:37).

What is more, the temptation that confronted Abram was very plausible. In taking Hagar as his wife, Abram was motivated not by lust, but by an eager desire to see God's purposes fulfilled. After all, though the promise had identified him as the father, Sarai had not yet been explicitly designated as the mother of Abram's descendants. Furthermore, the taking of a concubine was a socially accepted custom in that day. All parties involved were consenting adults, so why not? The idea seemed so reasonable, as Satan's shortcuts always do!

Look at the shortcuts that Satan offered Jesus in the wilderness: "Why don't you make these stones into bread? Otherwise, you may die of hunger, and that would hardly forward God's plan! Throw yourself down from the top of the temple, showing yourself to be the one who comes gloriously on the clouds. Otherwise, the people may despise the humble manner of your coming to earth, and thus miss out on the blessing you came to bring. You are going to appear that way someday, so why not now? Take possession of the world's throne now. Otherwise, you may end up with nothing but a cross. Isn't the crown yours by right anyway?" (cf. Matt. 4:3–10). Satan's proposals all seem so sensible. They seem to achieve God's purposes by a shortcut. But if you give in to Satan's wiles, you will discover, like Abram, that the shortcut doesn't lead you where you want to go.

I remember very vividly driving across America shortly after my wife and I were married. At one point in our journey, I was navigating and I suggested that we turn off the main road to follow a shortcut. So we did. Some time later, in the early hours of the morning, we found ourselves lost in Rockford, Illinois. To make matters worse, the town seemed to have abolished all road signs. It seemed like an eternity before we got back onto the right road. Ever since then, whenever I suggest taking a shortcut, a strange expression comes over my wife's face. She has learned that my shortcuts may be short, but they don't necessarily take us where we want to go! That's an attitude we should all develop toward Satan's shortcuts.

THE DIFFICULT WORK OF WAITING

Abram, however, was in too much of a hurry to see God's purposes fulfilled. Of course, *hurry* is a relative term, and probably not one that would have occurred to Abram. After all, he had been living in the Land of Promise for ten years already (Gen. 16:3).

An attitude of impatience and distrust is intensely dangerous. You are eager to see events unfold and have grown weary of waiting for God to act. You are anxious to see the way ahead, instead of walking by faith. You want to see every obstacle removed immediately. Perhaps you long to be married or to have a child or to progress to a more fulfilling level in your career. Yet you seem stuck at a dead end, with no apparent prospect of seeing your hopes and dreams realized. What should you do when the promises of God seem slow in being fulfilled? Certainly you may need to examine your own motives and obedience and to search your heart for hidden sins. Sometimes the desires of our hearts are turned in entirely wrong directions. But what do you do when it seems that the desires of your heart are good and proper, yet they remain as unfulfilled as ever? You must continue to wait for God's timing. God is not slow—but neither is he in a hurry.

Those of us who have very young children know how difficult waiting can be. We live through their annual anguish of waiting for birthday parties. Each day of the week—or, in some cases, the month—before their birthdays roll around, they wake up with the question, "Is it my birthday yet?" Finally, the great day arrives, and you immediately have to convince them that 6:30 A.M. is not the ideal time of day for a party. By 6:45 A.M., they are thoroughly convinced that you don't love them, and that all this talk of a party is nothing but a cruel hoax. At this point, you know it's going to be a long day!

Don't we often act toward God like little children? We kick and fuss and scream because we want what God has promised, and we want it *now*. Never mind that preparations need to be made and that other people need to be invited. But, like a patient and long-suffering parent, God bides his time, neither delaying nor hurrying, until everything is in place. Then—and not a moment sooner—he gives us the good things he has promised.

THE WRONG SOLUTION: HAGAR THE EGYPTIAN

Instead of waiting for God's time, however, Abram listened to his wife and took her maidservant, Hagar, as a concubine. Documents from the ancient Near East show that this was a regular custom in some societies, and some premarital agreements actually stipulated that a barren wife was to provide her husband with offspring in this way. But the same documents also bear witness to the likely costs of such relationships, providing laws to deal with the situation in which the concubine bears children and falls out of favor with her mistress. In other words, the domestic problems of jealousy, reproaches, and broken relationships that ensued in Abram's family were common occurrences. Hagar became pregnant and proud, Sarai felt despised and proceeded to make Hagar's life miserable, and Abram quickly sought to wash his hands of the whole business.

We human beings love to excuse ourselves. We are always making excuses and blaming someone else. We had a dog in England who frequently misbehaved. When caught with his nose in the garbage, he would look as guilty as can be. He knew that he shouldn't have been doing that. But he never once pointed the paw at someone else and said, "It was all his fault. He made me do it." Only humans do that, and this essentially human characteristic came quickly to the fore in Abram's previously happy household. Sarai blamed Abram for the whole mess: "You are responsible for the wrong I am suffering" (Gen. 16:5). Abram wanted Sarai alone to take full responsibility for what happened to Hagar: "Your servant is in your hands. Do with her whatever you think best" (16:6). Hagar was caught in the middle and responded by running away.

WHOSE FAULT WAS IT?

What a mess! Do you see what happens when you follow Satan's shortcuts? Sin so often seems to offer freedom, but you end up in even greater entanglement than ever. Sin offers a way of escape—but only out of the frying pan and into the fire! So whose fault was it? Was it all Abram's fault? Was it really Sarai's fault? Or was it Hagar's fault? The truth resists easy answers. We are all both sinners and sinned against. Abram should have been exercising godly leadership in the family, but the temptation came to him initially through Sarai's suggestion. Sarai, in turn, had no business turning against her maid, since pregnancy was the intended result of her idea. Yet in spite of that, Hagar owed proper respect to her mistress. This was not merely a matter of observing the appropriate social etiquette: verse 4 tells us that she "began to despise" her mistress—the same word that is used in Genesis 12:3, where blessing is promised to those who bless Abram, but a curse is pronounced on those who despise him. Surely enough, Hagar's disdain ended up with her wandering in the wilderness. All three people were sinners and all three were sinned against, just as in so much of our own experience.

Inevitably, the weakest comes out of it the worst. Hagar ran away and headed for her original home in Egypt. She ended up in the wilderness of Shur, on Egypt's northeastern frontier. This apparently insignificant geographical note draws our attention to a continual undercurrent in the story of Abram: the conflict between the attractions of Egypt and the apparent barrenness of the Promised Land. This theme first appeared early in Abram's story. He no sooner entered Canaan than he found that land unable to support him: "Now there was a famine in the land" (Gen. 12:10). The solution that occurred to Abram was straightforward: there is food in Egypt, so why not go down there for a while? Egypt appeared fruitful; the Promised Land was barren.

Similarly, in Genesis 13:10, the land chosen by Lot is described as being "well watered, like the garden of the LORD, like the land of Egypt." This area, at least on the fringes of the Promised Land, if not outside it, was, like Egypt, more attractive than the real thing.

And now we meet Hagar, whose Egyptian origins are emphasized in the story (16:1, 3). Not surprisingly, she was fruitful, while Sarai was barren. And when living with Abram's family became intolerable, Hagar headed for Egypt.

In each of these instances, however, choosing the fertility of Egypt over faithfulness to the promise led to disastrous consequences. Abram's journey down to Egypt nearly resulted in the loss of Sarai. Lot's choice of fertile land like Egypt nearly ended in his destruction, first when the kings of the East came calling (Gen. 14), and later when God's judgment fell upon Sodom and Gomorrah (Gen. 19). Hagar's son, Ishmael, was not just a continual problem for Abraham and Sarah; his descendants would also be a perpetual thorn in Israel's flesh. Hagar herself, in attempting to run away to Egypt, found herself not in a land flowing with milk and honey, but on her own out in the wilderness. The Egyptian option, while initially attractive, always led to disaster in the long run.

THE EGYPTIAN THEME IN GENESIS

To understand the significance of Egypt in Genesis, we need to remember that the book was written at the time of the Exodus, for people who were tempted to return to Egypt. In the wilderness, they quickly tired of manna and wanted to return to the more varied diet of Egypt (Num. 11:5, 18, 20). When the spies returned from their exploration of the Promised Land with a discouraging report, the people's first response was, "Wouldn't it be better for us to go back to Egypt?" (Num. 14:3). When there was no water to drink, they said, "Why did you bring us up out of Egypt to this terrible place?" (Num. 20:5). To them, the prosperity of Egypt must have been a constant magnet as they faced the difficulties of taking possession of the Land of Promise. But Genesis warned them that to return would be disastrous.

Similarly, Hagar's flight to Egypt was not the right option. To abandon Abram meant abandoning the blessing that was to be found in him. Yet, tragically, it was the behavior of Abram and Sarai themselves that led Hagar to flee. That raises a question for us: What kind of people are we? Do we draw people toward Jesus Christ or repel them? Are we an open door to the gospel or a barbed wire fence? Is it not true that all too often the church is the biggest obstacle in the way of people becoming Christians?

HAGAR'S BETTER FRIEND

Hagar was fortunate. In the wilderness, she met a better friend, the angel of the Lord. Like Eve before her, she found that her sin and failure were not the end of the story. The Lord was out there in the wilderness looking for the wanderer. In his gentle but firm approach, the angel of the Lord provided a classic model for evangelism: with a few brief words, he convicted Hagar of her sin of rebellion, pointed out the helplessness of her condition apart from Abram and his house, and assured her of both safe passage on her return and future blessing. Hagar was promised a son who would be great, the first of many descendants. In this gracious encounter by the well, we are reminded of another woman who met the Lord beside a well, the woman of Samaria (John 4). She too found that the Lord saw right through her, even to the depths of her sin, yet was still seeking to turn her into a true worshiper.

Like Israel in Egypt, Hagar cried out in her misery and was heard by the Lord (Gen. 16:11; cf. Ex. 3:7). Indeed, in Sarai's oppression of her Egyptian maid there is a miniature picture in reverse of the suffering and oppression that Israel would later undergo in Egypt. But the similarities between Hagar's situation and the later one of the Israelites only highlight the difference between the commands that the Lord gave concerning each. Whereas God said to Pharaoh, "Let my people go!" he said to Hagar, "Go back to your mistress and submit to her" (Gen. 16:9). One had to find freedom by leaving the house of bondage, while the other could only find freedom by reentering the house of bondage. Hagar was sent back simply because there was no blessing to be found apart from Abram and his seed. Painful though the way of submission may have been, there was no other way for Hagar to receive the blessing of God.

But Hagar's blessing would prove to be a continual problem for Israel. Her son, Ishmael, would live in the wilderness "close to" or "in hostility to" (the Hebrew can mean either one) his brothers (Gen. 16:12). He would constantly be in his brother's face, we might say. Sin always complicates things, and the effects are often lasting. There is no neat and tidy way of disposing of Abram and Sarai's sin. If there were, then there would be no need for the cross. Sin cannot be buried. It can only be atoned for. And there on the cross, we see in Jesus the God who really sees, who is looking out for the wanderer, pursuing us out in the desert. We see Jesus silently convicting us of our sin and rebellion against God, for which he hung there, but also pointing us to the way home, the way to blessing. There is no way to blessing that bypasses the cross. There was no shortcut for Jesus, and there is none for us.

So Ishmael was born. The promised child had not yet

come. We have to wait a little longer to see Isaac make his appearance. Man by his best efforts cannot bring about the fulfillment of the promises of God. Abram and Sarai disobeyed God, and their sin would have lasting consequences for their descendants. Yet Abram did not end up a failure. We don't remember him as the man who failed, but as the man of faith. The reason for that is that God is faithful, even when we are unfaithful. Abram's righteousness came not from himself, nor even from his faith, but from the God of whom his faith laid hold. So it was that Abram's failure did not frustrate God's plan. God had entered into a covenant with Abram and had vowed to take upon himself alone the curse of disobedience. That is precisely what he did for us in Jesus on the cross. Our failures, like those of Abram, were laid upon him, so that his righteousness might be credited to us. That's good news for Abram the failure and Hagar the wanderer—and it's good news also for you and me.

FOR FURTHER REFLECTION

1. Why was it wrong for Abram to have a child by Hagar?
2. How did the "solution" of a child actually increase Abram and Sarai's problems?
3. What name did Hagar give to God—and why (Gen. 16:13)?
4. Have you ever been tempted to take matters into your own hands because you thought that God was taking too long to answer your prayers? What warning signs should you be aware of as you choose between right and wrong actions?
5. What are some of the unexpected sources of temptation that have been a problem for you in the past?

7

OUR COVENANT GOD

(GENESIS 17)

What can you count on in this world? Who can you really trust? Surveys increasingly show that we don't trust anybody these days. People don't trust their spouses, their bank managers, their doctors—and we certainly don't trust the politicians. So whom *can* you count on these days? In our contemporary society, is there anybody who remains constant, who is true to his word, who can be trusted absolutely? The Bible says that there is: God. God is eternal, unchanging, and absolute.

That's all well and good, but how can I be sure that God will be there *for me?* What if I make some mistakes and make a mess of my life? What if I've spent my whole life running from God? What if I let God down? If I come back to him, will he still receive me? How can I know? As one songwriter put it,

> Surely this is cloudy water for turning into wine,
> Surely the most sour and bitter of the grapes
>   upon your vine.
> I don't mean to sound ungrateful Lord you know
> But even with the strength I've found,

In all your power and goodness Lord, there must
    be some mistake.
For I am weak Lord, so very weak Lord,
And I will only let you down.[1]

These are the kinds of doubts and questions that the
next part of Abram's story deals with. Tired of waiting for
God to fulfill his promise, Abram gave in to his wife's
nagging and had a child by her maid, Hagar. He really
made a mess of things this time. So much for the great
man of faith! Abram was eighty-six years old when Ishmael was born. Thirteen years later, he was wondering if
he still had a future in God's plans. Was there still hope
for this man who had fallen short of God's standards?
Genesis 17 answers that question resoundingly in the
positive. God's covenant with him was renewed. The
promises made in chapter 15 were still in force. There
was still a future for Abram. Why? Because our God
keeps his covenant with his people.

COVENANT RELATIONSHIPS

At this point, we need to explain a little more about
what we mean by a covenant. People back in those days
would have been familiar with the idea of a covenant,
but the idea is not so familiar to us today. Essentially, a
covenant is *a relationship based on the surrender of control.* We explained in an earlier chapter how a covenant
could be made between a big, powerful nation and its
weaker neighbor, offering protection in return for loyalty
and obedience. That neighbor had a choice: either surrender, enter the covenant, and receive the benefits of it,
or try to remain independent and face the prospect of an-
nihilation. Similarly, God told Abram that he was willing
to be his covenant overlord, offering blessings and ex-
pecting loyalty.

What is the practical application of this? What does it mean when we say that our relationship with God is based on a covenant? In the first place, it means that we cannot set the terms of our relationship with God. The terms of the covenant are not negotiable.

Imagine the weaker king in an ancient covenant saying to the great king, "Fine. Let's do a deal here, but I want to be in charge in this relationship. I want to say what you can do and what you can be like—and don't come making demands of me." It's absurd, isn't it? He would have found his head on a pole and his limbs distributed to the four corners of the empire before you could say "Assyria rules, okay!" Yet many people think that they can strike their own private bargains with God. They say, "I like to think of God as . . ."—as if they can decide what God will be like. They want to pick and choose what they will believe and what they will do—and they certainly don't want a God who makes too many demands on them. "My God isn't like that," they will tell you. In other words, they don't want a God who is *God*.

The real question, however, is not what you would like God to be like, but what he is really like. And he has revealed himself as the God who has made a covenant with his people. When the great king comes and offers to establish a covenant with you, you really have only two choices: you can accept the covenant relationship on his terms and receive its benefits, or you can refuse it and face the consequences.

Many people approach religion as if they were interviewing God for a job, the position of "personal deity in my life." "I want to find a philosophy that works for me," they say. But if God is really who he claims to be, *Almighty God*, then that is what he is, whether the idea "works for you" or not. You can interview idols and ideologies, but the God who created the universe offers you only two choices: surrender on his terms or face the consequences.

THE BENEFITS OF THE COVENANT

What are the benefits of the covenant that God offers? In its most basic form, God states the covenant like this: I will be your God, and you will be my people (Gen. 17:7–8). God offers us a relationship with himself. If you are not surprised by this offer, then you fail to appreciate just what God is saying. You are still thinking that you have freedom to pick and choose whom you will serve. You are still thinking in terms of interviewing God for a job: "Of course God would be delighted if I decide to let him be my God; it's what he's there for." But the whole point of the book of Genesis up to this chapter is that because of sin, there is no "of course" about it. In the Garden of Eden, a close relationship with God was a natural part of life. But afterwards, because of sin—the desire that each of us has to be in control of his own life and to choose for himself what is right and what is wrong—there can be no such automatic acceptance by God. The way back to the Garden, to God's presence, is barred by cherubim wielding a flaming sword (Gen. 3:24). Only God can tell the guards to stand aside.

That was Cain's problem: he thought that God should have accepted his sacrifice no matter what the attitude of his heart was. *It's God's job to accept sacrifices; he has no business picking and choosing whom he will accept and whom he will not,* he thought (see Gen. 4). This was also the problem of the builders of the Tower of Babel: they thought that if they all worked together, they could make their own way back to God through the construction of their wonderful tower. In their arrogance, they thought that it was going to reach up to the heavens (Gen. 11:4). They would burst in on God and surprise him—and of course God would accept them. That's still what most people think today: if I live a decent life and am nice to most people most of the time, then of course God will accept me—it's his job.

In fact, the reverse is true. If my own righteousness is all that I am relying on, then I have no hope of finding favor in God's sight. This is perhaps the hardest part of the Christian message to get across to people—the fact that we are not automatically headed for heaven. The truth is that our sin—not just the wrong things that we have done, but the very attitudes of our hearts—drives us away from God. That's why the gospel has always been better received among the prostitutes and drug addicts and losers than among the rich and famous. These people don't find it hard to believe that they have nothing to offer God. What about you? Have you reached the point in your life where you recognize that you have nothing whatever to offer to God? Do you recognize that there is no "of course" to his loving you, that his grace to you is truly amazing? If not, then you have never understood what lies at the heart of the Christian message. You've never understood that God delights in turning cloudy water into wine and stony ground into a fertile vineyard. The apostle Paul states the principle like this: "God chose the foolish things of the world to shame the wise; God chose the weak things of the world to shame the strong . . . so that no one may boast before him" (1 Cor. 1:27–29).

That's a lesson that Abram had to learn through his failures. Over the thirteen long years between the end of Genesis 16 and the beginning of Genesis 17, he had plenty of time to reflect on his own unfaithfulness to God. He had time to think about his own failure. So he was well prepared to recognize and appreciate the graciousness with which God came to him. In spite of everything, the Great King appeared once again to the man who had let him down, and confirmed his covenant with him. God's promises are not destroyed by man's failure, for our God is a God of grace.

It is their failure to recognize this need for grace that leads people to want a God who won't change their lives and who won't make demands of them. But that is not what God is offering in his covenant. He offers *himself*, and you can't have a relationship with him without it changing your life. It makes sense when you think about it. After all, you wouldn't expect to get married without it modifying your life at all. Imagine someone saying to you, "Oh yes, I'm married, but I don't let it affect my life. I do what I want with my money and my time. No, I don't spend time with my wife. Yes, I talk to her occasionally, but only when I really need something from her." You would think that was a pretty strange way to behave—yet people think that they can behave that way with God. They want God to be their God at least so that when they die, he will take them to be with him in heaven, but they don't show the least desire to be with him or his people now! They don't want a relationship with God that changes their lives. But that is the only kind of relationship God offers. God will be your God and come into your life and change it completely—or he will not be your God at all, with all the consequences that has.

CHANGES FLOWING FROM THE COVENANT

If you do recognize your own sinfulness, your own utter need of God, and the amazing grace that he shows in being willing to enter into a relationship with you at all, then you will be prepared for God to change your life. You need to be prepared for change, for when God does come into someone's life, he changes it completely. Look at Abram and Sarai: what did it mean for them to submit to God? First, God changed their names: from Abram to Abraham, and from Sarai to Sarah (Gen. 17:5, 15). When a covenant was made in the ancient world, it was common for the great king to give a new name to the lesser king (cf. 2 Kings 24:17). What a demonstration of control over someone! God was changing the most personal thing about Abram and Sarai, their names. What would happen if you went to work on Monday morning and said, "By the way, don't call me Jim anymore. God told me that I am to be called Fred, instead"? Imagine the reaction you would get! People would want to know what kind of weird cult you were mixed up in. But obedience to the God of the Bible is all-consuming. From then on, every time their names were spoken, Abraham and Sarah would be reminded that they were not their own, but belonged to God.

Furthermore, as a sign of his submission to the covenant, Abraham was now to be circumcised. This was no "Sunday only" kind of religion, which occupies an hour of your week and leaves the rest of your life up to you. This was a faith that penetrated even to the most personal areas of Abraham's life in a most painful way. What about you? Does your faith govern every area of your life, even the most personal and intimate? Does your relationship with God govern your sexuality? Does it govern your truthfulness at work and at home? Does it control the things with which you fill your mind, the ambitions and desires of your heart? If you are in a covenant relationship with God, then no area of your life can be unaffected. As Paul puts it, "We take captive every thought to make it obedient to Christ" (2 Cor. 10:5).

This is where the current debate over morality falls apart. People are continually saying on television and in the newspapers that we should be teaching our children morality. But what morality should we teach them? And whose values should we instill? We may all agree that we shouldn't murder each other. Our children receive strong messages on the danger of drugs from their schools. But what about extramarital affairs, people living together without being married, or homosexuality? "That's none of your business," we are told. Or what about people telling lies in order to sell products and boost their business? That's excused as being "just the way the business world works." Most people are in favor of morality—but only so long as it stops short of interfering with their lives. They want a morality that stays out of certain areas of their lives. But that's not what Christianity offers. Christianity is total surrender to the covenant God, a relationship so all-consuming that it controls every area of our lives.

CIRCUMCISION

Circumcision was not merely a painful test of Abraham's spiritual commitment, such as requiring him to pierce his ears, or lie on a bed of nails for a week, would have been. Circumcision was a covenant sign, a sign that involves cutting, just like the cutting up of the animals in Genesis 15. There the curse of the broken covenant was symbolized by animal carcasses, starkly demonstrating the destruction that would come upon the covenant breaker. God himself passed alone between the pieces, symbolizing the fact that he himself would pay for any breach of the covenant. In Genesis 17, however, the sign of judgment was applied to Abraham's organ of reproduction. This was the source both of the hoped for, promised seed and also of Abraham's failure involving Hagar. Turning the sign into reality would merely mean applying the knife a little more extensively, cutting off Abraham's seed. If Abraham failed to keep the covenant, his seed would be cut off.

When Isaac, the child of promise, was finally born, the token judgment of circumcision almost became a reality. Abraham was instructed to take him up onto a mountain, bind him on an altar, and offer him as a sacrifice. As Abraham stood with his knife stretched out above his beloved son, a voice from heaven told him to stay his hand. A ram would take the place of Abraham's seed on the altar. All of this points forward to the cross, the place where Jesus Christ would take upon himself the curse of the covenant in all its awful fullness. There, Jesus would bear the reality of judgment for sin to which circumcision pointed. As God in human flesh, Jesus fulfilled the picture of Genesis 15; as the seed of Abraham, he fulfilled the picture of Genesis 17. He was cut off for our sin, which enables our relationship with God, threatened by our sin, to stand.

CHOOSING YOUR RELIGION?

This relationship with God is a relationship that affects your children also. I meet many people who tell me that they want their children to be free to decide for themselves what they think about religion when they grow up. One lady told me that she keeps books from a cult alongside the Bible on her children's bookshelf, so that they will be free to make up their own minds when they get older. But the message of the Bible is that we are not free to choose our own gods in the way we choose our favorite brand of laundry soap. It is not simply a matter of "finding the religion that works for you"; it is a matter of surrendering to the covenant-keeping God or facing the consequences. When God chose Abraham, he didn't choose just him; he chose his children as well. God is not only the God of Abraham, but also the God of Isaac and Jacob. That is why Abraham was to circumcise his children: they needed to know that they were not free to choose their own gods. They were to receive the sign of the covenant to show them that they were part of the covenant people. They belonged to the one true God, and they were to submit to him.

Did circumcision save them? Absolutely not. Ishmael was circumcised on the same day as Abraham (Gen. 17:26), yet he showed no evidence of a heart renewed by grace. Although he bore the sign of the covenant, he was not ultimately part of God's covenant people. As he grew up, he lived "in the face of" God's covenant people (16:12), not in friendship with them. As Genesis 17:19–20 makes clear, although God's blessing rested on Ishmael and his descendants, his covenant was with Isaac and his descendants. In a similar way, circumcision pointed Israel's children to the one covenant God who alone could save them. If they trusted in him, like their father Abraham, they would find a refuge in him. But if they refused that God and rebelled against him, their very circumcision would testify against them. They too would be cut off as Ishmael was.

CIRCUMCISION AND BAPTISM

In the church to which I belong, we baptize infants. Why do we do that? Will baptism save your little Freddie? No. But it points him, as it points all of us, to Jesus Christ, whose cleansing blood is symbolized by the water. It points him to the need for a change in him that can only come from outside, for baptism, like circumcision, can be done to you only by someone else. Baptism also points him to the fact that he is part of God's covenant people. He is not free to choose his gods as he pleases; he must surrender to the one true God or face the consequences of eternal separation from him in hell.

But baptism is more than that. It is an act of faith in the promises of God. When Abraham circumcised his children, he knew that it was a circumcision of the heart that counted, not an external ceremony. They needed not simply to be warned of the dangers of hell, but to be cleansed. Similarly, when we baptize our children, we know that a baptism of the heart, a new birth through the Holy Spirit, is necessary. But in baptism we lay hold of the goodness of God, and claim for our children the promised Holy Spirit. By faith, we lay hold of Peter's declaration on the day of Pentecost, "The promise [of the Holy Spirit] is for you and for your children" (Acts 2:39).

Think about it: what grounds do you have for hoping that your child will receive the Holy Spirit and grow up to be a Christian? Perhaps you will say, "Well, I'm trying to do all the right things. I send him to church; I read the Bible with him; I set him an example in Christian living." I hope you do all of those things; they are a great blessing. But don't you see? The only thing that you can do for your child by yourself is make him or her religious. Only God can give little Freddie the new heart he needs. "Well, of course he'll do that," you say. But there is no "of course" about it. The only thing we pass on to our children as a matter of course is a sinful nature and a flawed example.

However, our God has revealed himself as a covenant God who deals faithfully with us as families, not just as individuals. That is what we proclaim joyfully to the world when we baptize little ones: that they too can look to our God in repentance and faith and receive the promised Holy Spirit. We are acknowledging to ourselves and to our children that we cannot save them—but also that God can, and will, if they look to him in repentance and faith, because he is a covenant-keeping God who does not change. God's promise remains sure because it rests upon his character and not upon ours.

Whom can you trust in this uncertain world? Whom can you count on? Our covenant God. Whom can you trust with your life? Our covenant God. Whom can you trust with your children? Our covenant God. But there can be no half-hearted obedience with this covenant God. He wants to enter into an all-consuming, life-changing relationship with you. He wants to remake you, to alter every area of your life into his image, so that you can live with him forever. Those are the terms of the covenant. Your only choice is whether to accept the terms, surrender to God, and receive the blessings he offers, or to face the consequences. As your children grow up, you are to re-mind them of the day of their baptism. You should say to them, "You are not free to go whichever way you choose. You need to repent and turn to Jesus Christ in faith and receive the new life that he offers." You need also to pray—and you can pray with boldness because you serve a covenant-keeping God—that God will grant your child new life in him. But search your own heart also. Are you yourself part of God's covenant people? Perhaps you have grown up in the church; perhaps you have been baptized, and assume that you are a Christian. But do you have the life-changing relationship with God that Jesus Christ came to bring? Or will you be left to face the conse-quences?

FOR FURTHER REFLECTION

1. How did God introduce himself when he ap-peared to Abram? What did he ask Abram to do?
2. Why did God give Abram a new name? What do the names Abram and Abraham mean?
3. Did the covenant blessings affect Abraham only? Why is it significant that God promised to be Abraham's God and the God of his descendants as well?
4. How does the biblical understanding of God, as the covenant initiator and covenant keeper, go against popular views of God in our society?
5. For Christians, how is it true that we must accept God on his terms or accept the consequences?
6. God displayed ownership of Abraham's life by changing his name and requiring circumcision. How does he display ownership of your life?

8

GOD'S FRIEND

(GENESIS 18)

"From a distance, God is watching us." So goes a line in a song popularized by Bette Middler,[1] expressing a common conception of what God is like. God, so the idea goes, is "somewhere out there," keeping a benevolent but distant eye on everything that goes on. Is that how you think of your own relationship with God? Abraham certainly didn't think in such terms. Over the past few chapters, we've examined many facets of his life. We've encountered Abraham the prophet, Abraham the priest, Abraham the king, and Abraham the failure. In this chapter, another aspect of his life receives attention: Abraham *the friend of God*.

ABRAHAM, THE FRIEND OF GOD

Abraham is the only person in the Old Testament to receive the title "friend of God" (2 Chron. 20:7; Isa. 41:8). Striking, isn't it? Abraham the failure became known as God's friend. How did that happen? The answer is, as every Christian knows from his own experience, by the amazing grace of God. Only grace—free, undeserved grace—can enable an imperfect person to dwell in the presence of the perfect God. Only grace permits the unholy to approach the Most Holy and be called his friend. God's relationship with those whom he has created is not limited to giving the distant, tolerant smile that you might bestow on an earnest, hard-working spider. Rather, he wants to call us his friends. This is the astonishing message of the New Testament. The relationship that Abraham had with God in the Old Testament is now opened up to you and me. Jesus said to his disciples,

> You are my friends if you do what I command. I no longer call you servants, because a servant does not know his master's business. Instead, I have called you friends, for everything that I learned from my Father I have made known to you. (John 15:14–15)

What's so special about a friend? A friend is someone to whom you open your heart. A friend is someone who knows not just what you are doing, but why you are doing it. Abraham, the friend of God, was the man to whom God opened his heart and with whom he shared his thoughts.

THREE MYSTERIOUS VISITORS

One day Abraham looked up and saw three mysterious figures coming out of the shimmering noonday heat. It was not a pleasant time to travel in the Middle East, and Abraham made them welcome, as any good host would. He brought out the best he had and set it before them; they sat down and ate, while he waited on them. Thus far, not much was out of the ordinary run of everyday life. But gradually the identity of these visitors began to become clear. First, the leader made a promise to Abraham that only the Lord could carry out: "I will surely return to you about this time next year, and Sarah your wife will have a son" (Gen. 18:10).

Any great ruler can promise to give land and riches to his favorites. But only God is able to guarantee offspring. Even in our technologically advanced age, we can make no such guarantees. What is more, this stranger knew everything; he demonstrated his omniscience by uncovering Sarah's secret laughter of doubt. She thought that she was safely concealed in the inner part of the tent, observing everything without being observed. But this stranger knew her most private thoughts (vv. 12–13). It is no surprise, then, that this mysterious visitor identified himself as the Lord (v. 13).

Throughout their encounter, the Lord treated Abraham as his friend. He shared an intimate occasion with him, a common meal. This was a unique privilege for Abraham. It was the only case before the Incarnation in which the Lord ate food set before him. There were certainly many other occasions on which the Lord appeared to people and they offered him food. However, on all those occasions he turned the food into a sacrifice. But with Abraham he enjoyed a special relationship. He sat down at his table and ate with him. Furthermore, while his two companions went on ahead to investigate the sad state of affairs that existed in Sodom, the Lord lingered and spoke with Abraham face-to-face about the events that were to follow.

THE PURPOSE OF THE VISIT

So what was the purpose of the Lord's visit to Abraham? It was not merely a social call, to pass the time of day. In the first place, the Lord was confirming the promise he had already made to Abraham. Abraham was told that a date had been set for the long-awaited birth of a son: a year later (18:10). But such a specific date was also a test of faith. It is one thing to believe that at some time in the future God will give you a child. It is quite another to fix your hopes on a specific date and risk a cruel and bitter disappointment if the event does not come to pass. Perhaps that is why Sarah found it so hard to believe. She laughed to herself, not daring to hope that what was promised might be true.

Yet the center of her doubt lay in something that God had promised to Abraham back in Genesis 17:16—that she herself would bear Abraham's son. Had Abraham been unable to convince her of that good news? Had he perhaps held back from sharing that particular piece of news with her, reluctant to raise hopes that might prove false? In any event, she seemed to be a reluctant believer, like so many of us. Sometimes God's good news seems just too good to be true. Even God's word was initially unable to break through her doubts. She laughed at God's promise, and then denied her laughter. But God saw right through her denials, just as he does with our excuses. Nothing can be hidden from him. He cannot be deceived.

The good news is, however, that God is more gracious than we expect. God had already been gracious with doubting Abraham (Gen. 17:17). His initial reaction had been just as incredulous as hers. Now the Lord was gracious to Sarah also, gently reaffirming his promise to the beloved doubter. His words were spoken in the same tone of voice as the gentle words of Jesus to Peter when he was overcome by the waves while walking on water: "You of little faith, why did you doubt?" (Matt. 14:31). This was not the response of a God who watches from a distance, remaining coolly detached from the efforts of his struggling creatures. You don't have to be afraid to tell God the truth about how you feel. He knows all your doubts, your fears, your dreams, and when you spread them out before him, he deals with them gently and graciously, as with a friend.

The Lord was not there simply to reveal to Abraham and Sarah their own future. He also brought Abraham into his deliberations concerning Sodom. Abraham was, after all, a prophet, and in the Bible the Lord regularly announces his plans in advance to his prophets (see Amos 3:7). This is especially true when judgment is impending. People must know that the judgment that has befallen the wicked is not simply a natural disaster or an accident of fate.

But the knowledge that there is a God in heaven who will act against the unrighteous brings with it great responsibility: Abraham was instructed to direct his own children and his household to keep the way of the Lord (Gen. 18:19). It is important to notice the order in which God does things. First came grace, as God said of Abraham, "I have chosen him." Abraham was not chosen because of who or what he was, but so that he might become what God wanted him to be. After grace there must follow obedience, through which grace reaches its goal. Moreover, Abraham was chosen not simply for his own benefit, but for the benefit of his descendants and household after him, as they would walk in the ways of the Lord. This is precisely the pattern we saw in the previous chapter: God sovereignly came to Abraham and graciously confirmed his covenant to his undeserving vassal. But that vassal was then obligated to respond in obedience, and to train his family to follow in the same path. Divine choice does not remove the need for divine command. Grace was not transmitted automatically to Abraham's offspring, but rather, as a general rule, through godly parenting. Abraham was directed to instruct his children properly, so that "the LORD will bring about for Abraham what he has promised him" (v. 19). The same assurance is given in Proverbs 22:6: "Train a child in the way he should go, and when he is old he will not turn from it."

This verse does not guarantee that every child started off on the right path will eventually become a Christian. Rather, the proverb holds us responsible to train our children in the ways of the Lord. In the mysteries of providence, the Holy Spirit commonly works through the influence, teaching, and discipline of godly parents from the earliest of days.

LOT'S FAMILY

The same message is illustrated in reverse by the example of Lot's family. His wife, reluctant to abandon Sodom even in the face of its destruction, turned back and was destroyed with it (Gen. 19:26). His sons-in-law thought that all the talk of impending judgment on Sodom was a joke (v. 14). His daughters, while leaving Sodom with him, took its depraved mind-set along with them into their new life (Gen. 19:30–38). Being a relative of Abraham did not provide automatic protection against God's judgment.

That lesson should not have been lost on the first readers of Genesis. Judgment could fall on disobedient Israel as easily as on unrighteous Sodom and Gomorrah. Their fate was a warning to Israel not to ignore the reality of the judgment to come. When Moses was looking for an image to express the possibility of complete destruction befalling the people in the event of their rebellion against the Lord, it was to the doom of Sodom and Gomorrah that he drew their attention (Deut. 29:23). When judgment falls on others, all too often our tendency is to be complacent and regard it as a well-deserved punishment on particularly bad people. The truth is rather that we all deserve to be destroyed like that. The inhabitants of Sodom and Gomorrah may have been more brazen in their sin than you or I, but ultimately we all face the same prospect. As Paul says, "We must all appear before the judgment seat of Christ, that each one may receive what is due him for the things done while in the body, whether good or bad" (2 Cor. 5:10).

This truth motivated Paul to be diligent in his efforts to persuade people to be reconciled to God (2 Cor. 5:11). Similarly, knowing that judgment was about to fall upon Sodom and Gomorrah, Abraham interceded with the Lord, humbly but nonetheless effectively. He interceded not simply for his own needs and those of his house, but for the wicked city. The friend of God was also the friend of sinners. He was not a friend of sinners in the way that Lot was, so hopelessly compromised with them that there was little that was distinctive about him. His friendship with sinners led him to intercede on their behalf. Like Paul, he desired that they should be saved, and his desire led him to pray. This raises a question for you and me: Do we earnestly pray for the wicked—not simply those whom we regard as "good prospects" who might be comparatively easily won over, but the out-and-out wicked? Do you intercede for your local equivalent of Sodom and Gomorrah, or only for your good friends?

ABRAHAM'S "HIGH PRIESTLY PRAYER"

In his prayers, Abraham didn't claim his own merit or standing before God as the reason why his requests should be granted. He recognized that he had none: he was but "dust and ashes" (Gen. 18:27). Whereas Jesus would in his High Priestly Prayer refer to his own authority and glory in the presence of the Father (John 17:2, 5), Abraham appealed simply to God's just character: "Will not the Judge of all the earth do right?" (Gen. 18:25). However, Abraham didn't suggest that God would be unrighteous to take vengeance. In our own day, there are many who think that Sodom and Gomorrah should have been spared, not because of their goodness, but because evil doesn't really deserve judgment. By contrast, Abraham simply argued that it would be unjust to include the righteous in the fate of the wicked.

Nor was Abraham concerned merely with the temporal fate of the righteous. He was not simply worried that a few good people might get swept away in the fall of Sodom. That could be prevented by removing them from the scene of destruction, as eventually happened. And even if they were not rescued, their permanent fate was secure. All too often, the righteous do suffer along with the wicked. Rather, Abraham was concerned with the possible leavening influence of the righteous. As long as a sufficient number of righteous people remained in Sodom, the possibility of the conversion of the wicked remained a reality. As in the parable of the wheat and the weeds (Matt. 13:24–30), Abraham was concerned that premature destruction might root out the Lord's harvest.

Was that why he stopped his intercession at ten righteous men? It was not that he got tired of arguing with God, but rather that a minimum number of righteous people was needed to have that leavening effect. That number was later laid down as the minimum necessary to form a synagogue. A city can be so far gone that even the most righteous people in its midst will not save it. Such was the case of Jerusalem in Ezekiel's time: according to Ezekiel, even the presence of such luminaries as Noah, Daniel, and Job would not have saved it (Ezek. 14:12–23). As Zvi Adar sums it up,

> So long as there are righteous men the wicked may be pardoned in the hope that good will eventually prevail. In the absence of any righteous man, mercy shown to the wicked would only encourage and reinforce their wickedness.[2]

Even Sodom, for all its wickedness, need not have been destroyed if only ten righteous men had been found in it.

That's the difference a few people on fire for the gospel can make. As long as there is a remnant, there is hope, and so Abraham interceded.

Ultimately, however, Abraham rested his case on God's righteousness. He remained confident that the Judge of all the earth would do the right thing. He didn't seek to usurp God's right to be the Judge of all the earth. He didn't make demands on God, and he received no specific promise. The case may indeed have been hopeless. The only solution may have been to mark for salvation those who were mourning over the abominations, as in Ezekiel's day (see Ezek. 9:4). But as he looked at the cup of wrath about to be poured out on Sodom and Gomorrah, it was as if he said, "Father, if it be possible, let this cup pass; give more time for repentance; yet not my will but thine be done." Yes, he was God's friend, given the privilege of interceding for the lost, but he recognized that he was not God. God, the just Judge, is the only one who is able to bring about the salvation of the ungodly.

How does a just Judge save the ungodly? He does that through Jesus Christ, Abraham's greater descendant. Jesus did not simply intercede on behalf of his unrighteous people; he himself took the cup of wrath in their place, so that grace might be shown to them—and even to such a place as Sodom. Abraham's intercession for Sodom was not unavailing; even though Sodom itself was destroyed, God remembered Abraham and rescued Lot (Gen. 19:29). How much more may we be certain that the high priestly intercession of Jesus will be effective! God remembers the sacrifice of Jesus on the cross and in consequence is rescuing an uncountable host from the wrath to come.

CAN THIS CITY BE SAVED?

Now if a place as wicked as Sodom could have been saved, then anyone can be saved, no matter what his background. But could a place as wicked as Sodom really have been saved? Astonishingly enough, the answer of the Bible is yes! There's a fascinating passage in Ezekiel 16 that describes in graphic detail the wickedness of Jerusalem and the judgment coming upon it. Jerusalem is portrayed as more wicked than Sodom, the home of sexual abominations, and worse than Samaria, the home of idolatry. What an indictment: God's holy city is shown to be worse than those twin towers of corruption! But then Ezekiel goes on to speak of a restoration—a restoration not only for Jerusalem, but one that includes Sodom. The home of proverbial unrighteousness and the home of the temple will both be restored together. Why? God's answer in Ezekiel is this: "When I make atonement for you for all you have done, you will remember and be ashamed and never again open your mouth because of your humiliation" (Ezek. 16:63).

There's no room for pride when salvation is entirely a matter of grace; it can reach down to Sodom as easily as to Jerusalem. Sodom was to be destroyed, but it can be restored. Even though Sodom was the very height of wickedness, it is not beyond the reach of God's grace. Why? Because the death of Jesus Christ, the righteous for the unrighteous, is an all-sufficient atonement for the salvation of the very worst sinner. In the words of Frances van Alstyne,

> The vilest offender who truly believes
> That moment from Jesus a pardon receives.[3]

Yet we also have to recognize the other side of the gospel. The wickedness of Sodom, left to itself, is inevitably doomed. Wickedness will be judged. The people of Sodom had been rescued earlier by Abraham (see Gen. 14), but now the ax was beginning to descend. This time even Abraham's intercession would not save them. Their sin cried out to heaven for punishment. The fact that the

Judge of all the earth would certainly do right is not good news, but bad news to those who are wicked.

In Genesis 18, we have before us two different peoples. On the one hand, there are the people of faith, joined to Abraham, receiving the gracious promises of their God, who deals patiently even with unbelief. On the other hand, there are the children of wrath, facing certain destruction. We see Abraham pleading on behalf of the unrighteous, that they may be saved. Surely Abraham was praying for their salvation, not simply for more time in which they might prolong their sin. But ultimately Abraham also recognized God's absolute right to judge.

Time ran out for Sodom—but it has not yet run out for us. We may still intercede for our friends and family, recognizing God's right to judge, but pleading the merits of Christ. No one is beyond the reach of his blood. If Christ's death on the cross was enough to redeem wicked Sodom, then it is enough for the worst sinner today. That should give you a holy boldness, combined with holy humility, in bringing those around you before God's gracious throne. For we too have the privilege of being called God's friends.

FOR FURTHER REFLECTION

1. How did Sarah respond to the renewal of the promise? Why?
2. Did Sarah's doubt and denial thwart God's plan? How is that a comfort to you?
3. In Genesis 18:23–25, what is the basis for Abraham's bold pleading on behalf of Sodom? Is God's just character good news or bad news?
4. How does Abraham's pleading on behalf of corrupt Sodom form a model for our own attitude toward the godless pagans we meet today?

9

THE TITANIC SINKS
(GENESIS 19)

In the 1970s, there was a popular series of disaster films that went by the title *Airport!* The basic plot was very predictable. You knew even before the opening scenes of the film that however peaceful and routine the flight appeared, this would be no ordinary trip. A tragedy was inevitable. Similarly, everyone who saw the recent hit movie *Titanic* knew from the outset that the ship would sink. Disaster films are, by definition, like that. The catastrophe is certain.

Similarly, the cities of Sodom and Gomorrah have been doomed ever since they were introduced in Genesis 13 with the ominous words, "This was before the LORD destroyed Sodom and Gomorrah" (Gen. 13:10). The reason for their destruction was also given a few verses later: "Now the men of Sodom were wicked and were sinning greatly against the LORD" (Gen. 13:13). From that point on, just as in a disaster film, the only question has been, "When will the catastrophe befall them?" In Genesis 19, we finally reach the equivalent of the point in the movie where the plane slams into the mountain or the ship hits the iceberg. This is the end of the road for Sodom.

Now that the disaster has begun, there is another question to be answered, as devotees of disaster films will recognize: Can anyone possibly be saved? The answer in the movies is, invariably, yes. Our interest lies in seeing how it is done and how many will make it out alive. In Genesis 19, we wonder if anyone will be saved out of Sodom—and if so, how? This concerns us far more directly than any disaster movie, for the broader background of the fall of Sodom is the universal wickedness of humanity begun in Genesis 3. It was not just the inhabitants of Sodom who "were wicked and were sinning greatly against the LORD." From Adam and Eve onward, all of the people whom God created to know him rebelled against him. In consequence, everyone has been exiled from the Garden of Eden and placed on a "Titanic" of a world. On this excursion, some may travel first class, living superficially wonderful lives, while others may travel steerage, eking out their days in misery. Either way, every person who has ever lived is on an inevitable collision course with judgment. Will anyone be saved out of the destruction of this doomed planet?

LOT'S PROGRESS

Over the course of the past few chapters, we've followed Lot's "progress." At first he was a rich nomad, too prosperous to dwell in the same place as Abraham. When they separated, he chose the most promising-looking place to live; however, it was just on the edge of the Promised Land, if not already outside it. What is more, he swiftly went from living "near Sodom" (Gen. 13:12) to living "in Sodom" (14:12). As a result, he needed to be rescued by Abraham when a foreign army carried off the inhabitants of Sodom. But Lot still didn't learn his lesson. He apparently assimilated even further, and gained a position of authority and standing in the community, for he sat in the gate (19:1), the place where community decisions were made. His daughters were engaged to be married to men from Sodom, and he owned a house there. He had come to regard the Sodomites as his "friends" (19:7). Lot had become a settled man of substance, yet compromises must have marked his rise in the community. You can't live comfortably in a place of such wickedness as Sodom without compromise.

But even while he compromised, the spark of his faith was not utterly extinguished. He is still called "righteous" in the New Testament. Why? Because he grieved over the wickedness around him. The apostle Peter describes Lot as "a righteous man, who was distressed by the filthy lives of lawless men (for that righteous man, living among them day after day, was tormented in his righteous soul by the lawless deeds he saw and heard)" (2 Peter 2:7–8).

Lot never totally identified with the world in which he lived. Yet, at the same time, he was unwilling to leave it behind. He was, as Derek Kidner calls him, "the righteous man without the pilgrim spirit."[1] How many of us are like that? We're Christians, yes. But we also want to have our part of the world. We must have our slice of the action. We feel that we can't possibly give it up completely: that would simply be too great a cost to bear. So, like Lot, we seek instead to do our best in a hopelessly compromised situation, trying to maintain dual citizenship in the world and in heaven.

It doesn't work. Look, for example, at Lot's attempt to rescue the angels. He pressed them with more than usual vigor to accept his hospitality. The alarm that was evident in his voice (Gen. 19:3) shows that he knew what might happen to them otherwise. He knew that the streets of Sodom were not a safe place to spend the night. Yet even his best efforts were not enough to protect them. All the men of Sodom, both young and old, came to his house and demanded that he hand the men over to them to be abused. He found himself in an impossible situation. The only way he saw to fulfill one sacred obligation, to protect his guests, was to betray an even more sacred obligation, to protect his daughters. He was caught between a rock and a hard place, with no way out. How often does that happen to you? You find yourself in an impossible dilemma because of past compromises with sin. Sin has a way of doing that to you. It complicates everything and puts you into untenable situations. Too late, you say to yourself, "How on earth did I get myself into this—and how can I get myself out?"

TIME TO RUN

The answer in Lot's case was, "You can't get yourself out." Only the intervention of the angels—dazzling the men of Sodom—saved him from an awful fate. Enough! The sins of Sodom were complete. Now the time had come for judgment. The ax had begun to fall. Was Lot unwilling to leave Sodom before, because he thought that the cost would be too great? Now he had to leave if he wanted to save his life, even though it would cost him everything he owned. Depart or perish! That's the thing about our schemes to hold onto a slice of the world; they have a way of backfiring. We end up hoisted with our own petard. Lot was about to discover for himself the truth of the old saying, "You can't take it with you."

At least he had a chance to take his family. He pleaded with his sons-in-law to come with him, but even a desperate last-minute appeal in the dead of night would not convince them. He had apparently never spoken to them before about divine judgment, so why should they listen to him now? It all seemed like some crazy kind of practical joke to them. Before it was too late, the angels grabbed Lot's hand and the hands of his wife and two daughters, and led them out of the city. It was a scene reminiscent of the opening pages of *Pilgrim's Progress*: Pilgrim, stick your fingers in your ears and run, though it seems to all the world—even those nearest and dearest to you—that you have taken leave of your senses. There was an urgency in their flight.

Have you sensed that urgency yourself in spiritual matters? Do you convey that urgency when you speak to your friends and family members about things to come? Do they know that you are in dead earnest about eternity? Do they know that you have staked everything on the reality of the wrath to come and the salvation offered in Jesus Christ? Total commitment is necessary. It is not enough to be on the run. It is not even enough to be on the run in the right direction. Many people were willing to fall in with Pilgrim for part of the journey to the celestial city. But when the going got tough, many dropped out. Pliable was eager to leave the city of destruction on the strength of Pilgrim's description of the joys of heaven, but as soon as they fell into an awful bog, the Slough of Despond, he got cold feet and turned back. It's not enough to go part of the way with the pilgrims. It's all or nothing; a full commitment is necessary. That is what Lot's wife discovered. In spite of the angel's warning, she looked back. A remnant consisting of only four people was saved from the destruction of Sodom, and one of those four disobeyed the angels' command and was consumed along with the city. She didn't have the commitment to go all the way, and so she perished. Where is your heart? On what are your eyes fixed? Are they fixed on the city that is to come, or do they keep glancing longingly back at the city you have left behind?

THE RELUCTANT PILGRIM

Having said all that, it needs also to be added that it is not the commitment that saves, but the Lord. Look at Lot: even with the brimstone raining down around him, he was still a reluctant pilgrim. He was utterly unable to fulfill the conditions that the Lord laid down for his salvation. He complained that he couldn't flee to the mountains, and instead he pled for an extension of God's grace. Was he still reluctant to leave the worldly ways of cities behind completely? Did he still have to have an earthly city, even if only a little one, to make life bearable? What a miserable picture he presents! But see also how patient, how gracious, God is. God held back his entire timetable of destruction so that he could save poor, compromised Lot. For the sake of Abraham and because of his intercession on Lot's behalf, Lot was not destroyed.

It's tempting for us to be arrogant and to think that we are so much better than Lot, but are we really? Are we less compromised than he was? Are we less attached to the things of the world? We are not saved because we are wiser or holier than others, or because God considers us to be above-average human beings. Like Lot, we don't even have the strength to escape right! Only God's grace, extended to us because he has decided to save us, is enough. Knowing our weaknesses, Jesus Christ has interceded for us, just as he did for Simon Peter, so that our faith may not fail us (Luke 22:32). God will not allow that intercession to fail, nor will he allow his intention to save a people for himself to be frustrated.

Judgment is suspended until the righteous are safe, but then the ax falls. There is no room for complacency. The Lord waits so long in his graciousness that people think he cannot judge, but when he does come in judgment, it is so decisive that it seems as if he cannot show mercy. For this is not the sudden anger of an irritable temper, easily inflamed but equally easily pacified. This is deliberate, measured wrath, following a full investigation of the facts. There can be no last-minute appeals or reprieves, for there is no higher court to whom appeal can be made, and no pertinent facts have been overlooked in reaching the verdict. So it was with Sodom and Gomorrah, and so it shall be at the end of history. In fact,

Jesus specifically compares those days to the destruction of Sodom in Luke 17:28–30.

> It was the same in the days of Lot. People were eating and drinking, buying and selling, planting and building. But the day Lot left Sodom, fire and sulfur rained down from heaven and destroyed them all. It will be just like this on the day the Son of Man is revealed.

On that day, judgment will fall without mercy on the ungodly. But there is for us now, as there was for Lot, a little place of refuge to be found. A narrow gate that leads to life has been opened up for us in Jesus. How was Lot saved? He was certainly not saved by his wisdom or his righteousness. Rather, he was saved by God providing a place of refuge for him. So it is also for you and me. We too are not saved by our own goodness or wisdom, but by taking refuge in the goodness of Jesus Christ, given to us as we trust in him. There is no other hiding place, no other safe refuge from the final outpouring of the wrath of God against sin.

THE JUDGE OF ALL THE EARTH ACTS

Early the next morning, Abraham went back up to the place of intercession to see what had happened to Sodom and Gomorrah. Did he doubt God's ultimate willingness to judge? Was he perhaps hoping for a last-minute miracle of repentance, such as would happen to Nineveh in Jonah's day? Could a God of grace really destroy his own creatures, wicked though they were? One look at the rising cloud of dense, black smoke gave Abraham the answer. It was the answer that Abraham already knew, for he had said it himself: "Will not the Judge of all the earth do right?" (Gen. 18:25).

But isn't this only an Old Testament view of what God is like? People in those days may have thought of God as wrathful and judgmental, but doesn't the New Testament depict a different picture of God? Not at all. We have already pointed out that Jesus himself draws the parallel between the fate of Sodom and the final judgment of the world in Luke 17. In Old and New Testament alike, God is depicted as both just and gracious. But how is it possible for him to be both? The answer is found in the cross. There God's wrath and justice were satisfied. God judged sin, putting to death the sinless Son of God for the sins committed by his people. There too, however, God's grace was equally on display. There God's mercy was freely offered to all who would come to Jesus Christ in repentance and faith, trusting in his goodness and not their own. There on the cross, perfect justice met perfect mercy. The words of William Rees's hymn capture it exactly:

> On the Mount of Crucifixion fountains opened
> deep and wide;
> Through the floodgates of God's mercy flowed a
> vast and gracious tide.
> Grace and love, like mighty rivers, poured inces-
> sant from above,
> And heaven's peace and perfect justice kissed a
> guilty world in love.[2]

What is more, the judgment executed on Christ puts to death any thought that God could otherwise forgive sin. Unless there was no other way for us to be redeemed, the cross makes no sense. Consider this analogy: Suppose I saw a huge truck thundering out of control toward you, about to crush you under its wheels. If, out of my friendship for you, I threw myself in front of it to save your life, you would be filled with gratitude. But suppose I threw myself under a truck simply to demonstrate my love for you when you were in no danger. You would more likely interpret such a bizarre act as a sign of severe mental instability than of love. Only if there is no other way of preserving life is a sacrificial death heroic. Otherwise, it is a foolish waste, a merely romantic gesture. Similarly, if there was any way to save the world other than by Jesus' death on the cross, then his death was unnecessary and foolish. Would not a viable alternative make a mockery of Jesus' own agonized words in the Garden of Gethsemane: "My Father, if it is possible, may this cup be taken from me" (Matt. 26:39)? The cup was not removed, for there was no other way.

A NEW LOT?

Was Lot reformed by his experience of judgment and salvation? Hardly. You can take Lot and his daughters out of Sodom, but it's a lot harder to take Sodom out of them. Living alone with his daughters hardly led to renewed righteousness. Once again the temptation came from within his own family circle. His daughters' biological clocks were ticking, and they wanted children. There is nothing inherently wrong with that, but, as with Abraham and Sarah in Genesis 16, they were unwilling to leave the future to God. There was something that was more important to them than obeying God. They wanted children who would carry on the family name, and they were willing to do whatever it took to achieve that goal.

Yet are we so different from them? Have you never said to God, "I must have a husband (or a wife) for my life to be meaningful"—or "I must have children," or "I must have a career," or "I must have good health," or whatever? If there is anything in your life that you *must* have, apart from God, then it is your idol. When push comes to shove and you have to choose between serving your idol and serving God, then you will find out where your real commitment lies.

Lot's idol was wealth and comfort, and so he chose security and prosperity over the Promised Land. Ironically, in spite of his choice, he ended up with neither security nor prosperity. The story ends with him living in a cave, not even in control of his own body. His daughters, on the other hand, received what they sought: sons to carry on the family name. Yet though they satisfied their idols, were they ultimately any better off than their father? Their future descendants, with some exceptions—notably Ruth—remained outside the covenant community, outside the promises of God. In contrast to Lot and his daughters, Abraham chose God plus nothing, trusting in the bare promise of God. He ended up with more than he asked for: the seed through whom salvation would come to the world—even though he did not see all of God's promises fulfilled in his own lifetime.

What is particularly striking and tragic is that neither Lot nor his daughters returned to Abraham. The problem of Lot's prosperity had been radically dissolved by God; like the Prodigal Son, he now had literally nothing to stand in the way of his return home. The angels had directed him to flee the plain and return to the mountains, the place from which Abraham looked down to see the judgment of God unfold on Sodom and Gomorrah. Yet even after Lot finally did abandon the plain and leave the halfway house of Zoar behind, and return to the mountains, he still did not seek out the one person in whom blessing could have been found: Abraham. Even when he was deprived of finding satisfaction from his idols, he still was not willing to return in repentance to the way of God. So he ended his days in misery and depravity, a sorry shell of what he once was.

Which of them are you most like? Are you like the inhabitants of Sodom and Gomorrah, comfortably set in your sins, oblivious to the ticking time bomb of God's judgment? Are you like Lot's wife, ultimately unable to give up the world for God? Are you more like Lot, believing in God, yet compromised and compromising for the sake of something you want more than God, hardly able to be saved? Or are you more like Abraham, living by faith in God's promises in the midst of this world of much tribulation, looking to God for salvation and trusting him to bring you to the city that is yet to come?

FOR FURTHER REFLECTION

1. What does the destruction of Sodom and Gomorrah teach you about God's attitude toward sin? Does God still punish sin today? If so, how?
2. Describe how Lot's location changed after he left Abraham.
3. Lot's decision to live in Sodom, surrounded by depravity, put him in a terrible dilemma—whether to protect his guests or his family. How do the effects of sin, yours and others, complicate your life and put you in compromising situations?
4. Why was Lot so hesitant to leave Sodom? How did the angels finally get him to leave the city?
5. How far is God willing to go to persuade you to leave your sinful life behind? In what ways has God shown you his grace against your will?
6. Are there times when you act as Lot's wife did, looking back on your old sin-filled life with longing and wishing you didn't have to leave it behind? How does this attitude affect your relationship with God?

10

TWO STEPS FORWARD,
ONE STEP BACK
(GENESIS 20)

Sometimes, when a horse is learning how to jump over fences, it comes to one that it refuses to jump. It sticks its ears back and its nose down, it digs its hooves in, and will not jump. What do you do in those circumstances? You walk the horse around for a while to calm it down, and then you take it right back to the same fence. If necessary, you do it over and over again until finally the horse sails over the fence, as it should. Abraham needed to learn that God can be trusted to take care of him. He needed to learn that lesson well, because there would be an exam, a test of his faith, coming up. God would take him back to the same hurdle over and over again, so that he would be prepared to jump over it with flying colors.

CAN GOD DELIVER?

In this chapter, we find God taking Abraham back to the beginning, back to precisely the same hurdle at which his faith had faltered earlier. The scenario was very similar to that related in Genesis 12:10–20. On that occasion, famine in the Promised Land had led Abraham to go down to Egypt. On his arrival there, he was afraid that Pharaoh might kill him in order to marry Sarah, and that fear led to his failure. He told Sarah to pretend to be his sister, not his wife, and as a result Sarah almost ended up in the harem of a foreign king.

Now the whole cycle was reenacted, and Abraham fell into exactly the same trap all over again. The issue was really still the same one that we saw in Genesis 16, when he gave in to the temptation to seek a son through Hagar, and it is an issue that is familiar to many believers. The question with which Abraham struggled, just like so many of us, was this: Can God keep his promises without any help from me?

In contrast to Lot, who settled down to a life of compromise with the inhabitants of the land, Genesis 20:1 shows us that Abraham was still an alien in the Promised Land, moving from place to place. He had not forgotten that this world was not his home. So far, so good. Yet his lifestyle was not without its dangers. As he wandered around without the protection of a clan structure or an overlord, the possibility of exploitation or even death at the hands of those in whose land he lived was always there. This risk was probably especially high whenever he moved to a new area. Significantly, in Genesis 20:1 we find Abraham going farther south and west than before, into the region of the Negev. He was now wandering on the fringes of the Promised Land, which always seemed to be a place of danger for the patriarchs.

In any event, any relocation inevitably leads to a time of uncertainty. In many instances, transitions provide opportunities for temptation. When you are uprooted and have to deal with a whole new set of circumstances and people, you tend to go back to habitual ways of dealing with problems. Those habitual ways are very often wrong! Abraham was often afraid that someone would kill him and marry Sarah. That was not an unreasonable fear in his circumstances; it was not unheard of for those with power to use it to steal from the powerless. But to deal with his fear, he had developed a strategy of lying about her identity. As verse 13 makes clear, this was not merely an occasional lapse under pressure; it had become a regular *modus operandi*. Abraham had instructed Sarah, "Everywhere we go, say of me, 'He is my brother.'"

Shouldn't Abraham have known better than that? He had the promise of God. He was supposed to be living by faith. Whatever happened to his earlier attitude of "God said it; I believe it; that settles it"? Yet isn't that precisely the problem that faces most believers living in the reality gap? Our problem is not so much with the fundamental doctrines of God's sovereignty and care, or with the "big issues" of our walk with God. Rather, our problem is with the practical application of the promises of God to the details and difficulties of our daily walk. Yes, God has promised X, Y, and Z. I've memorized the verses to prove it. Yes, I believe it and proclaim it fervently on Sundays. But what about Monday morning, when, in the cold light of day, the situation looks distinctly unpromising? What about those times when obedience just seems too hard and faithfulness to God seems likely to cost too much? Then our memorized texts seem to disappear from our brains in a flash.

Once, when I was working as a maintenance mechanic during my seminary days, I was asked to clear up the workshop over the weekend. So I did. I threw out all the trash, including a stack of pornographic magazines that I found stuffed in the back of a drawer of tools. It seemed like a reasonable thing to do. Garbage like that undeniably belonged in the dumpster! I thought that nothing would come of it. But on Monday morning, I was called into the boss's office and I nearly lost my job. It was made very clear to me that my actions were unacceptable, and, under pressure from my workmates, what had seemed so clearly the right thing to do suddenly became less clearly so. I didn't change my mind about the value of pornography, but, in typically cowardly fashion, I did start to wonder if I should in the future take such a bold stand on the subject.

Have you ever experienced one of those Mondays? The temptation in that kind of situation is to think for yourself, instead of trusting God. It's so easy to add your own efforts to those of God, and then to substitute trust in your own solution for trust in God. It's so easy to say to yourself, "If I just bend a little bit to fit in, then everything will be okay." That was Abraham's problem, time and time again. He came up with his own creative solutions to the problem, instead of trusting God.

FOR BETTER OR FOR WORSE

There's something else to notice here, too. Though in Genesis 16, it was Sarah who was leading Abraham astray into unbelief, here in chapter 20 it was the other way around. Once again, we see temptation coming through the ones we love and trust. In fact, Abraham virtually blackmailed Sarah into adopting his strategy. He said to her, in effect, "If you *really* love me . . ." (v. 13). That is a hard appeal for anyone to resist. The truth is that we have an enormous impact on those around us, for good or evil. You can make it easier for them to live out their faith or you can make it harder. You can pass on to them an attitude of expectation and faith or an attitude of unbelief. Which of these describes you? Within the family circle, are you the one who guides others toward God? Are you a positive influence on your friends, or are you just "one of the gang"? Within your church, are you a spiritual leader (in the broadest sense) or a millstone? We have a responsibility as friends, spouses, parents, and church members to see that our presence brings people closer to God and does not lead them away from him.

And what is our influence on unbelievers? Abraham had an opportunity to have an impact on the lives of those whom he met. It was his calling, remember, to be a blessing to those around him (Gen. 12:3). Instead, Abraham thought the worst of those around him, and he responded by acting in a self-protecting way. He said to himself, "There is surely no fear of God in this place, and they will kill me because of my wife" (v. 11). Abraham's mistake was not that he was talking to himself. Far from it; that's precisely what he should have done. But he should have been saying to himself, "God has promised me a child through Sarah. Even though these people may be godless, God can still protect me. And if not, what is more important than obedience?" In other words, he should have reminded himself of the promises of God, the power of God, and his own commitment to God.

In the last chapter, we saw Lot's daughters giving in to the temptation to say, "If I can't have X, then God is not enough." They said to themselves, "We must have children if our lives are going to be meaningful. We can't get them in the usual way, so we'll have to get our father to lie with us." They had to choose between having children and living in obedience to God's law—and they chose children. Here, Abraham was saying that his personal safety was more important than obedience. If he couldn't have both, then he would choose safety. Safety, preserving his own life, had become his idol, just as obtaining children was an idol for Lot's daughters.

How many of us have similar idolatries? Perhaps your idol is control. So you say to yourself, "Lord, I trust you—but I need to know at all times how everything is going to work out." Or perhaps your idol is comfort. You say, "Lord, I'll go wherever you want me to go—but don't ask me to leave behind my nice home and pleasant lifestyle."

For another, it may be the opinions of other people: "Lord I want to witness for you—but only if I can do it without people thinking I'm an idiot." Whenever there is something more important to you than obeying God, you have set up an idol in your heart.

STANDING FIRM

By contrast, consider the attitude of Daniel's three friends, Shadrach, Meshach, and Abednego. In exile in Babylon, they faced death in the fiery furnace if they would not bow down to King Nebuchadnezzar's golden statue (Dan. 3). It would have been easy to give in and make at least a token bow, as so many others did, but they stood firm. Their response to Nebuchadnezzar was very significant.

> If we are thrown into the blazing furnace, the God we serve is able to save us from it, and he will rescue us from your hand, O king. But even if he does not, we want you to know, O king, that we will not serve your gods or worship the image of gold you have set up. (Dan. 3:17–18)

The three friends reminded themselves in the first place of God's power to save: he can close the mouth of hungry lions and quench the power of the burning fire. However, even if he chose not to do so, their commitment to him was such that they would rather burn than turn. Nothing was more important to them than obeying their God, even if it meant a painful death on their part. But even their commitment to doing the will of God pales in comparison to that shown by Jesus. In the Garden of Gethsemane, he prayed, "My Father, if it is possible, may this cup be taken from me. Yet not as I will, but as you will" (Matt. 26:39).

Oh yes, there was another way out. Jesus didn't have to suffer for our sins. But if he had not suffered and died, there would have been no salvation for us. The success of God's plan to redeem a people for himself rested squarely upon his shoulders. So Jesus chose the way of obedience to God's will, even to the point of suffering perhaps the most painful form of death ever devised by man. His commitment to God's plan of salvation was so great that he would voluntarily endure the agonies of hell that we deserved, in order to see that plan accomplished.

IS GOD GOOD?

Abraham didn't only doubt God's ability to protect him. He also started to question God's goodness. That doesn't come out quite so clearly in our English translations, but Genesis 20:13 literally reads, "When the gods caused me to wander. . . ." Abraham made his divine call to go to the Promised Land sound like nothing more than the aimless wandering of a refugee. Instead of witnessing to Abimelech about God's enduring faithfulness to him over the past twenty-five years, he talked like one pagan to another. Instead of speaking of God's goodness to him, in spite of his own failures, he talked as if his future lay in the hands of blind Fate. In his heart, he was starting to doubt that God was really good.

You can understand Abraham's feeling like that. He must have often felt that his life was going nowhere. That's the way life often feels when you are living in the reality gap. But isn't this Satan's prime strategy to woo us away from obedience to God? He used it successfully on Eve in Genesis 3. He tried it unsuccessfully on Job, believing that if he took away all of God's material blessings, Job would then curse God. Is it too much to say that a major cause of disobedience in our lives is our doubting of God's goodness? It causes us to covet: we say to ourselves, "If God really loved me, he'd give me what I want." It causes us to lie and cheat and steal and be sexually immoral. What we are saying in our hearts when we do those things is this: "I want something that I don't think I can get through obedience to God. I need it and God isn't giving it to me, so I'm just going to take it for myself."

Because so many of our sins flow from a basic doubting of God's goodness to us, trying harder and beating ourselves whenever we fail often doesn't change our pattern of behavior. For it doesn't deal with the root problem, the big sin behind the surface sins: our failure to believe that God is really good. In fact, the more pharisaical we get in our approach to life, the more we become convinced that God isn't really good. How could God really want the best for us, and then load us down with all these rules and regulations?

The real answer to sin is the gospel. It is remarkably straightforward. You need to look at Jesus on the cross and focus on the exchange that was transacted there. My sins were loaded on him, while his perfect righteousness was given to me. When I set that reality clearly before my eyes and understand it in my heart, how can I doubt that God is good? The road to joy-filled obedience begins when this great truth dawns on us: "He who did not spare his own Son, but gave him up for us all—how will he not also, along with him, graciously give us all things" (Rom. 8:32).

If I know—not just in my head, but in my heart of hearts—that God is good and has been abundantly good to me, then my heart's desire will be to obey this God who has loved me so much. Nothing will be more precious to me than pleasing this God to whom I am so precious. I may, and will, frequently fail to live up to the calling I have received. But as long as I remember his goodness to me, glorifying and obeying him will always be my passion and delight.

God continued to be gracious to Abraham. He didn't come down with a big stick and beat him up for failing again. He didn't say, "That's it! I've had it with you; I'm going to find someone else to fulfill my promises through. You've had your chance and you blew it!" No, God convicted him of his sin—but gently. He showed him tenderly just how wrong he had been about God, and also how he had been wrong about Abimelech. Originally, Abraham had thought to himself, "There is surely no fear of God in this place" (Gen. 20:11). But it turned out that Abimelech, the pagan king, did fear God. When God appeared to him in a dream and revealed to him that Sarah was Abraham's wife, he acted immediately to set things right. What is more, he summoned Abraham to explain his behavior. How humbling that must have been to Abraham!

Yet even Abraham's failures were used by God. This is a comforting truth for everyone who has ever really made a mess of a witnessing opportunity. Perhaps someone gives you a great chance to share the gospel with him, but you are afraid to say anything. Later on, you feel so bad. Or perhaps someone to whom you have been witnessing for months catches you in a lie or some other sin. You feel terrible about it. Yet God is still able to use an incompetent missionary. Even while Abraham was behaving irresponsibly, putting Abimelech at risk of committing a grave sin unknowingly, God was in control of the entire situation. He kept Abimelech from touching Sarah, preserving both her purity and his (Gen. 20:6). After Abraham was confronted by Abimelech, he finally became what he should have been all along, a blessing to the nations (v. 17). Abimelech was rewarded for his favor shown to Abraham; he and his household were healed. Sarah was returned safely to her husband, and Abraham was given even greater wealth than he had before!

But notice how God answered Abraham's prayers. After one simple prayer by Abraham, he opened the wombs of Abimelech's wife and slave girls, so that they could have children again. Yet after years of praying for a child of their own, Abraham and Sarah remained childless. How heartbreaking it must have been to them to see fertility return to Abimelech's household! But ironically, how encouraging it must also have been to see that happen, for the God who opened one closed womb could just as easily open another, even that of Sarah herself.

GOD'S LOVE FOR SINNERS

God's ability to use even our sins for his own purposes shows that he doesn't love us simply for the great things we can do for him. There's an additional verse to the children's hymn "Jesus Loves Me" that we don't sing very often, but that captures this aspect of God's love perfectly:

> Jesus loves me when I'm good,
> When I do the things I should.
> Jesus loves me when I'm bad,
> Though it makes him very sad.

All too often we think that in order for God really to love us, we must live a life of grand achievement. Surely we should go out as missionaries and convert whole nations and plant new churches among those who have never heard the gospel. Or at least we should win all of our friends and neighbors to the Lord. We typically focus on external achievements as the way to win God's approval: we want to attempt great things for him. The Bible, however, focuses on the internals: God's work of creating a great heart in us characterized by humility, gentleness, patience, and love.

Only this explains why God's plan so often seems at odds with our script for our lives, not just at our worst moments, but also at our best. It is not just when you are planning to go out and rob a bank that your car doesn't start. It is when you are minding your own business, doing your regular daily tasks. Or it may even be when you are trying to do something especially good for him. You finally pluck up the courage to go and share the gospel with your sister, and it is at that moment that your car won't start. That opportunity may be lost, but that doesn't mean that it was wrong for you to want to share the gospel with her. Similarly, when the computer eats the sermon I am preparing, it is not necessarily a sign that what I wrote was particularly bad! Sometimes when we attempt to serve the Lord, it doesn't work out successfully. And sometimes the examples are far from trivial. People go out to another land desiring to be faithful missionaries, and they are kidnapped and killed. How can God allow that to happen? Is God asleep at the wheel? Certainly not. He just has a different agenda from ours. You wanted to do great things for him in the world, but he wanted to make some small progress on his plan to do something great in your heart.

One of the ways in which he does that is by showing us, and others, our sin. Often that will be embarrassing for us, even humiliating, especially if we are in positions of Christian leadership. But in that way he gives us an opportunity to repent publicly, to speak plainly about the gospel that is the only hope for sinners like us. Jesus loves us when we are bad, as well as when we are good, and our public sins give us ample opportunity to testify to that amazing fact.

FOR FURTHER REFLECTION

1. What fear led Abraham to persuade Sarah to pretend that she was his sister, not his wife? Why was that fear unfounded?

2. How did Abraham's sin affect Sarah? How did it affect Abimelech and his household?
3. What did Abraham know about Sarah and her relationship to the blessing that made this sin worse than the one back in Genesis 12?
4. What sins are a recurring problem for you? How is God dealing with you concerning them?
5 Do you ever presume, like Abraham, that you are the only godly person around? In what surprising places have you discovered people who were unexpectedly more righteous than you?
6. What is God's attitude toward us when we fail time and time again, as Abraham did?

11

CROSSING THE RUBICON
(GENESIS 21)

Are you a "belt-and-braces" man? I don't know if there is a feminine equivalent to this British idiom, but a belt-and-braces man is someone who wears both a belt and a pair of braces (the British equivalent of suspenders) to hold his trousers up. That way, even if his belt breaks, he is still covered. In other words, he has an extremely cautious approach to life. He likes to have a strategy to deal with every possible problem before it occurs.

I can describe that kind of person well, because that's the kind of person I am, and I think Abraham was more than a little like that, too. As we have seen, he got himself into trouble on several occasions by trying to help God out. God had to take him over the same hurdle again and again until he learned that God could carry out his promises without his help. Abraham's strategies were always getting him into trouble, but God's faithfulness to his promise dug him out each time. Now in this chapter we finally see the promise fulfilled: the Lord did for Sarah what he had promised, and the child Isaac was born!

But the birth of Isaac did not finish the learning process for Abraham. Having reached this point by faith, the temptation was then to continue by sight. As we will see in the next chapter, Abraham would face the temptation to put his faith in Isaac, the promised child, rather than in God.

TWO KINDS OF LAUGHTER

The birth of Isaac was a moment of great joy; his very name means "laughter." No other name would do for such a long-desired and long-expected child. It had been twenty-five years since Abraham left Haran on the strength of God's promise. Now, at last, he began to see that promise fulfilled. Few events in the Bible, apart from the birth of Jesus, were so anticipated. Yet to most people the event must have seemed insignificant: a little baby was born to an elderly nomad—unusual, perhaps, but hardly earth-shattering. Only the eye of faith could see in Isaac the fulfillment of God's promise. Yet to those with eyes to see, to the people of faith, there was cause for great rejoicing in the birth of the child of promise (Gen. 21:6).

Not everyone was equally happy about Isaac's birth, however. To Ishmael, the birth of the baby was a cause not for rejoicing but for scorn. Ishmael laughed, too, but his was the laugh of unbelief, not that of faith. He was not laughing with Sarah, but at Sarah. He was mocking Isaac, and with him, God and God's promise. To him, the excitement surrounding the birth of Isaac was all a big joke.

We tend to ignore mockery of God. We see it so constantly all around us that it is hard to do anything else. Yet the Bible always treats mocking as a serious sin. For instance, in Psalm 1:1 the mocker is listed along with the wicked and the sinner as those with whom the wise man does not keep company. Indeed, in the book of Proverbs, the mocker is the opposite of the wise man (Prov. 9:8, 12). The third commandment, "You shall not take the name of the Lord in vain," warns us against treating God and his attributes lightly. Mocking God is so serious because it arises from an attitude of unbelief. Faith believes God and takes him at his word; mockery ridicules God's word and treats him with scorn. The person who holds such a position needs a total conversion—but the only thing that can bring about such a change is the very thing that is the object of scorn, God's word.

THE SLAVE WOMAN AND HER SON MUST GO

By adopting an attitude of scorn, Ishmael was declaring himself outside the promise of God. He sneered at the birth of a little baby, instead of bowing down before him, lost in wonder, love, and praise. Sarah would not tolerate such an affront to God and to the child of promise. She went to Abraham and demanded that the slave woman and her son be sent away. Since they had no interest in the true inheritance of Abraham, which was given to believers like Abraham, they had no place in his household.

Abraham was reluctant to agree to his wife's demand. At first we may be tempted to share that reluctance. Sarah's demand may seem harsh to us, even if Ishmael deserved it. Abraham's reluctance to force them to leave was certainly motivated, at least in part, by his natural affection for his son. Was he also, however, unwilling to rely entirely on the promise of God? After all, Isaac was but an infant. What if something happened to him? Child mortality rates were high in those days. Wouldn't it have been wise to keep Ishmael in reserve, so to speak? The belt-and-braces pragmatist was probably emerging at this point.

In this domestic dispute, however, God was on Sarah's side. As an aside, we have displayed for us here an important dimension of what it means to be a submissive wife. Sarah is held up as a classic example of submission in 1 Peter 3:5–6, but that does not mean that she was a doormat. She didn't stand around saluting her husband and constantly saying "Yes, dear. Whatever you say, dear." She was able and willing to confront Abraham when necessary. In this instance, the Lord supported not only her right to question Abraham, but also her view of what needed to be done.

For the sake of the promise, Abraham had to commit himself fully to Isaac (Gen. 21:12). Neither natural concern for the welfare of those whom he loved nor tentativeness on his part could be allowed to hold him back. Sometimes people hold themselves back from fully obeying the call of God because of family concerns. They say to themselves, "If I go out as a missionary, how will I find a spouse?" or "Who will take care of my parents?" or "What will happen to my children?" The answer is that God is able to take care of these things, as many can testify from their own experience. In the words of Jesus, "Seek first his kingdom and his righteousness, and all these things will be given to you as well" (Matt. 6:33). God answered Abraham's natural concern for Ishmael's welfare by promising that Ishmael's offspring would become a nation (Gen. 21:13).

Sometimes people hold themselves back out of fear. They want a reserve plan in case God's way doesn't work out. But God demands an all-or-nothing commitment to the promise. You can't keep a foot in both camps. So God repeated his promise to Abraham as the reason he should listen to his wife: "Listen to whatever Sarah tells you, because it is through Isaac that your offspring will be reckoned" (v. 12).

How would Abraham respond to the promise? He believed God, and so he sent Hagar and Ishmael away.

ISHMAEL'S FUTURE

What happened next was in many ways tragic. Cut off from Abraham's household, Hagar and Ishmael were devoid of sustenance. Abraham was the source of blessing; cut off from him, they were also cut off from the benefits that flowed through him. They could not support themselves, and they seemed to be in danger of dying. But God intervened to rescue them, in accordance with his promise to Abraham. He opened Hagar's eyes to see a well. Their physical needs were taken care of. They not only survived, but prospered, because God's blessing rested upon them for Abraham's sake.

Spiritually speaking, however, their condition was not so good. The boy became an archer and married an Egyptian girl. That may not seem like an important point, until you remember that throughout the story of Abraham, Egypt represents the temptation to abandon the Promised Land. Abraham went to great lengths to get a suitable wife for Isaac from among his own kinfolk. But Ishmael had no interest in the spiritual inheritance that he might have received from Abraham. He was content so long as his earthly needs were met. An Egyptian wife would do just fine for him.

So it is with so many people. They are satisfied if life merely goes well for them. So long as God takes away the big problems in their lives, they are happy. How different it might have been, though, if Ishmael had responded differently to the child of promise. On his attitude to Isaac his spiritual future stood or fell. On a different scale, it is the same for all of us: our spiritual future rests on our response to Jesus, the child of the promise. The rejoicing of faith leads to the path of blessing. The scornful laughter of unbelief may not lead to immediate physical disaster, but it means being cut off from God's richest blessing, the blessing of eternal life.

HAGAR AND SARAH

The apostle Paul picks up the imagery of this chapter in Galatians 4:21-31. He interprets it as an allegory. Hagar stands for those who depend on their own efforts to be accepted by God. They are in bondage to the law, and their standing before God is therefore inevitably temporary and precarious. Sarah, on the other hand, stands for those who are living by faith on the basis of the gospel. Such people are not trusting in their own righteousness, but in the righteousness of Jesus Christ, credited by God to their account. They are the children of the promise. Theirs is a liberty that Hagar could never know. Such people enjoy a permanent relationship with God, for they are not merely tolerated, but approved.

Hagar and Ishmael must have always lived under the threat of being sent away. They had no firm status in Abraham's household. Their presence there was always insecure. One blunder could, and ultimately did, cost them their place in the household. So it is also for those who rely on their good works. They can never have assurance of their salvation because they can never be sure that they have done enough to please God. But Isaac's place in the household, along with that of Sarah, was secure. They belonged. They were the objects of God's promise and could never be cast away. Likewise, those who rely on Jesus will never be cast away by God, for they are his adopted children, to whom the inheritance belongs by right. As John puts it, "To all who received him, to those who believed in his name, he gave the right to become children of God—children born not of natural descent, nor of human decision or a husband's will, but born of God" (John 1:12–13).

Into which of these groups of people do you fall? Are you a child of the slave woman or a child of the promise? How can you tell the difference between them? The key is in your attitude to the fulfilled promise of God in Jesus. When you think of Jesus, does it stir within you joy or scorn? What does Jesus' death on the cross mean for you? Does it fill you with joy as you see there God taking upon himself the penalty that you were unable to pay for yourself? Or are you rather insulted by the idea that your own goodness may not be enough by itself? The person living by faith gladly abandons everything else and clings to Jesus as the only source of his standing before God. He relies not on his belt and braces, but only on the promises of God fulfilled in Jesus. That's where your security must lie.

ABRAHAM AND ABIMELECH—AGAIN

In the second half of Genesis 21, we once again encounter Abimelech (21:22–34). Abimelech's earlier encounter with Abraham evidently made a strong impression on him, for he came to Abraham and sought to establish a lasting covenant with him and his descendants (v. 23). The pagan king recognized the hand of God at work, and he wanted to ensure that there would be no more falsehood on Abraham's part toward him or his descendants (v. 23). There was in this an implicit rebuke of Abraham for his previous actions, which undoubtedly did constitute falsehood on Abraham's part, yet Abimelech now wished to let bygones be bygones and move forward into an amicable future. Before that could happen, however, Abraham had a matter of his own to raise. Abimelech's men had seized a well that Abraham had dug; this injustice he wished to see resolved.

Both general and particular concerns were addressed in what followed. Abraham gave sheep and cattle to Abimelech, and together they made a general treaty. Then Abraham set aside another seven lambs from his flock; in accepting them as a gift, Abimelech was publicly recognizing Abraham's specific claim to have dug the disputed well. Thus, they all lived happily together—if not forever after, at least for a long time (v. 34). Abraham enjoys a period of peace and prosperity.

Abimelech once again provided a model of how the

kings of the earth should act toward God's people. Notice, for example, how different Abraham's relationship with Abimelech was in comparison to his relationship with the king of Sodom. Abimelech came to Abraham and found a blessing in him. Like the wise king of Psalm 2:10–12, he made his peace with the Lord and the Lord's anointed. Abraham was once again fulfilling his calling almost in spite of himself. But Abraham, too, was learning about God. He was learning that the Lord is the eternal God (v. 33). He is unchanging, from everlasting to everlasting the same, a God who may be relied upon. Because of God's intervention, Abraham found that the land about which he said, "There is surely no fear of God in this place" (20:11), turns out to be a land where he can dwell at peace for a long time. Appearances can be deceiving; but the promises of God stand forever.

FOR FURTHER REFLECTION

1. What does the name Isaac mean? Why was that such an appropriate name for Abraham's child?
2. In what ways was the birth of Isaac like the birth of Jesus? In what ways were they different?
3. List several reasons why Abraham did not want to see Ishmael go. Why was it necessary? What promise did God give Abraham concerning this son?
4. In what way did Ishmael's welfare depend on his response to Isaac? In what way does your welfare depend on your response to another child of promise, Jesus Christ?
5. What promise are you tempted to trust in today, instead of resting in the God of the promises?
6. What should a wife do today when she disagrees strongly with her husband?
7. What painfully difficult things does God ask us to give up? Why does he do that?

12

FAITH PUT TO
THE TEST
(GENESIS 22)

What is your top priority in life? What is it that you must have to be happy? We've been asking that same question several times over the past few chapters. What, apart from God, do you have to have to make your life meaningful? What's your idol? For Lot's wife, it was the city she left behind, Sodom. For Lot's daughters, it was children. For Abraham, in his encounter with Abimelech, his desire for safety won out over obedience. In effect, he was saying, "God is not enough; I must have safety as well." What is it in your life that you must have? Is obedience to God always your top priority, or is there some part of your life where you are not willing to say, as Job did, "Though he slay me, yet will I hope in him" (Job 13:15)?

This is not a decision that you make once and then it's over. It is a daily struggle. But we should be making progress, as Abraham was. He struggled over and over again with this question: "Am I willing to believe in God's ability to do what he has promised, without my help?" Was God able to take care of Abraham and Sarah when famine came? Was God able to open Sarah's womb?

STAKING EVERYTHING ON THE PROMISE

In Genesis 21, we saw the challenge to Abraham to believe that God would fulfill his promise through Isaac, and to stake everything on that. The proof of Abraham's faith was seen in his willingness to drive out Hagar and Ishmael, and thus abandon any notion that Ishmael provided a backup for the line of promise. Now, however, God put Abraham to the ultimate test (Gen. 22:1). That supreme test was whether he was willing to sacrifice Isaac, should God demand it. Everything until now had been preparation for this moment. Originally, God had called him to leave his closest relatives and go in faith to a land that God would show him. Now again God was calling him to go in faith to a place that God would show him. But this time the expected outcome of Abraham's obedience was not blessing, but the cutting off by his own hand of the one through whom blessing was to come. Probably none of us has ever had our faith put to such a severe test as was Abraham's faith, nor would we wish it upon ourselves.

How severe was the test? It was a test that touched his closest loved one. It is one thing to make a choice to believe God when you know that you are the only one at risk. But what if it means risking the lives of those whom you love? That would be so much harder. Not only that, but the test involved his only son, his beloved son (Gen. 22:2). But perhaps hardest of all, it was a test that involved the one through whom the promise was to be fulfilled. It was through Isaac that he was to have multitudes of descendants and to possess the Promised Land. Killing Isaac meant kissing God's promises good-bye. In the space of three short imperatives—"Take Isaac . . . go . . . sacrifice him" (v. 2)—Abraham's whole world came crashing down around him.

IDOLIZING THE PROMISE

Even the promises of God can become idols. As soon as you say, "I must have God plus the good things he has promised to his people," then God's blessings have become an idol in your heart. Job was a righteous man who served God with all his heart. God said to Satan, "Have you seen my servant Job? There's no one like him in the whole earth; he is blameless and upright." Satan responded, however, "Of course he serves you. You make it worth his while. You've given him everything he could wish for. But take everything away and he will curse you." So God did take everything away—and Job didn't curse him. Job never understood why it was happening. He never got to see the reason for all his sufferings, but he came to the point where he saw that what he wanted was God and God alone. He was able to say, "Though he slay me, yet will I hope in him" (Job 13:15).

The same case could have been made by Satan against Abraham. God blessed him with riches, posterity, and a great name. What had he really given up in comparison? Friends and family in Ur and Haran? Big deal! But now Abraham would really be put to the test. To kill Isaac would mean the end for God's promises—short of a miracle. The reader knows that this was only a test, but Abraham didn't. Did he serve God for God's blessings or for God himself? Was he willing to obey God even if it seemed that God was not going to honor his promises in this life? How about you and me? If God were to take away every possession that you own and with it your spouse, your family, and your friends, would you still serve him? What if there were to be no fruit that you could see from your life of faithful service to him? What if you were to pour yourself into sharing the gospel with people who ultimately rejected it, not once or twice, but for a lifetime? What if you were to be betrayed by those whom you most trusted? Are you willing to say, "If I have

God and God alone, I have everything I need for life and death"?

It is sobering to visit the graveyards of the pioneer missionaries. Many of those who went out to West Africa in the last century lasted only a few months. Some barely made it off the boat. What did they accomplish for God? What fruit did they see from their labors? There, in a distant land, they not only buried their dreams of ministry, but often also their wives and small children. They were willing to pour themselves and their loved ones out as a sacrifice to the Lord. Nor is that simply ancient history: the Christian radio station in Liberia where I worked for two years had its own small graveyard of missionaries, and the director of the mission had himself buried his own child in Africa.

By contrast, I once saw a film that depicted Hollywood's idea of contemporary missionaries trying to convert a tribe of Indians in the remote Amazon rain forests. There were many things wrong with that film's depiction of missionaries: the actors didn't talk like missionaries, they didn't pray like missionaries, and they certainly didn't act like missionaries! But for me, the greatest travesty came in a scene where the young son of the missionary couple had died of blackwater fever. As they buried him, his father cried out to heaven in a rage, "I did not give my permission for you to take my son!" In truth, many missionaries have recognized that God has the right to ask anything of them, and they have been willing to make the ultimate sacrifice out of obedience to God's call. They *did* give God their permission.

RESPONDING TO THE TEST

How does Abraham respond to the challenge placed before him? We are told that he got up early (Gen. 22:3). He set about obeying God right away. What is more, he didn't get cold feet as time went by. It took three days to get to the place appointed by God (v. 4). Those days must have seemed like an eternity to Abraham. Did he perhaps have faith from the beginning that God would somehow perform a miracle? His instructions to his servants may suggest that: "Stay here with the donkey while I and the boy go over there. We will worship and then *we* will come back to you" (v. 5). And when Isaac inquired about the lamb, Abraham assured him, "God himself will provide the lamb for the burnt offering, my son" (v. 8). But should there be no miracle, he was willing to carry through his obedience to the utmost, just like Daniel's three friends, Shadrach, Meshach, and Abednego, who would rather die than bow down to Nebuchadnezzar's idol (Dan. 3).

Abraham reasoned that God could raise the dead (Heb. 11:19), but he had no direct promise from God to that effect. He simply believed God and acted in obedience. His faith led to action. Once again he had returned to the point of saying, "God said it; I believe it; that settles it." Will not the Judge of all the earth do right, even if we don't understand what he is doing?

God called Abraham to go to the very edge in his obedience. Isaac was bound and laid on the altar, ready to be sacrificed. Again he had to take the knife to his son, just as he had on the day of his circumcision. Only this time the judgment would apparently not merely be a token, but absolute. But just at the point when the knife was raised, about to descend on his beloved son, the angel of the Lord called out to him from heaven.

> Abraham! Abraham! . . . Do not lay a hand on the boy. Do not do anything to him. Now I know that you fear God, because you have not withheld from me your son, your only son. (Gen. 22:11–12)

As Abraham looked up, he saw that God had indeed provided a lamb; there, trapped in a thicket, was a ram that he could offer as a sacrifice in his son's place. Abraham had passed the test. He had established once and for all that his hope was in a heavenly inheritance, not an earthly one. He had learned, again, that God was able to fulfill his promises without anyone's help.

"ABRAHAM SAW MY DAY"

Did Abraham learn anything else that day? According to Jesus, "Your father Abraham rejoiced at the thought of seeing my day; he saw it and was glad" (John 8:56). What did Jesus mean by that? I think he meant that Abraham had a unique insight into the way of salvation that was to be established through Jesus Christ. Surely this experience with Isaac was an essential key to gaining that insight.

In the first place, Abraham understood that there is no "of course" about God's promise. Some people take God's forgiveness for granted. They say, as did the philosopher Heinrich Heine, "God will forgive; it's his job." Actually, there are two ways in which you can say that. First, some people think that it doesn't matter how you live, because God will ultimately accept you anyway. They believe that a God of love would have to forgive everybody. Second, other people think that because of the good lives that they have lived, God owes them salvation. They expect a *quid pro quo* for their efforts: they have been good people, so God has to forgive their failings and welcome them into heaven. Abraham, on the other hand, recognized that God's promise was neither an automatic certainty nor a *quid pro quo*. He was willing to see the entire future blessing of the human race go out the window, if obedience to God required it. For that is what the sacrifice of Isaac would have entailed. The death of the child of promise would mean the end of the promised blessings. Abraham recognized that God was not under any compulsion to save large numbers of people, or even any, if he so chose. It is only because of his gracious commitment to his covenant promises that any are redeemed. Our God, as C. S. Lewis used to say, is not a tame God.

Second, Abraham now understood from his own experience the intensity of God's love for his people. For God did not spare his only Son, either, but gave him up for us all. It is one thing to understand the principle of painful sacrifice intellectually. It is quite another to stand there with the knife raised up in your hand, about to cut off forever the source of your joy, simply because God has asked you to do so. Abraham "gave God his permission."

Third, Abraham understood the principle of substitutionary atonement. Sacrifices in the Old Testament had a variety of meanings. Some were like tribute paid to an overlord. Some were freewill gifts, given by a thankful heart without any compulsion. Some had the character of a fellowship meal, with God and man seated together. Some, like the whole burnt offering that Abraham was told to offer Isaac as, were an expression of total self-consecration. But many Old Testament sacrifices also expressed the idea of substitution, and perhaps nowhere in the Old Testament is this aspect of sacrifice clearer than it is here. The ram takes the place of Isaac under the knife (Gen. 22:13). So also Jesus, the Lamb of God, takes away the sins of the world by going under the sword of God's wrath in our place.

Fourth, Isaac was restored again to his relationship with his father, but not without a sacrifice. His redemption could not be accomplished without the shedding of blood. God didn't simply call off the whole sacrifice after Abraham passed the test. The sacrifice still had to be made. Only the victim was changed. So it is also for us. Grace may be free to us, but it is so only because God has borne all the cost himself in Jesus. God has proved himself to be *Jehovah-jireh*, which means "The LORD Will Provide" (v. 14), because he has provided a substitute not merely for Isaac, but for all of us. Significantly, the place where he provided a substitute for Isaac was on Mount Moriah (v. 2), where Solomon's temple would later be built (2 Chron. 3:1), only a short walk away from Calvary, the place of the cross.

Fifth, while Abraham's faith in the promise of God led to his obedience, that obedience in turn led to a renewal of the promise. That is what we find in Genesis 22:16–18.

> I swear by myself, declares the LORD, that because you have done this and have not withheld your son, your only son, I will surely bless you and make your descendants as numerous as the stars in the sky and as the sand on the seashore. Your descendants will take possession of the cities of their enemies, and through your offspring all nations on earth will be blessed, because you have obeyed me.

God swore by himself—for there is nothing else by which he can swear—that what he had promised to Abraham would come about. Paradoxically, it is *because* Abraham was willing to put the promise on the line and risk losing it, that the promise was renewed. Had he clung to the promise in an idolatrous fashion, choosing the promise of God over the God of the promise, the promise itself would apparently have been placed in jeopardy. As Jesus put it, "Whoever wants to save his life will lose it, but whoever loses his life for me will find it" (Matt. 16:25). God can have no rivals for our affection, not even the good gifts and blessings he has given to us. Because of his faithfulness, Abraham would have not merely one descendant but many, and they would possess a land of their own, in spite of their enemies. What a comfort this repeated promise must have been to the wilderness generation, standing on the verge of entering the Promised Land. They must have been nervous about the fulfillment of the promise. At times, it must have seemed that God was calling them to a suicidal assault. But they too would learn what Abraham learned: that God would provide, one way or another, and that his promise would stand forever.

FOLLOWING THE LAMB

We may be called upon to give up many things for Christ, even the things most dear to us. You may lose people who mean more than life to you, or lose your dreams, and the parting can indeed be bitter. But we know that our God is able to raise the dead. Our inheritance is not on earth, but with Christ in heaven, where nothing can touch it. What is more, we have the precious promise of Jesus himself.

> I tell you the truth, at the renewal of all things, when the Son of Man sits on his glorious throne, . . . everyone who has left houses or brothers or sisters or father or mother or children or fields for my sake will receive a hundred times as much and will inherit eternal life. (Matt. 19:28–29)

In all of this, Jesus has himself forged the path. In the Garden of Gethsemane, two roads presented themselves. The soldiers had not yet come, while his disciples around him slept; he could still choose to decline the cup, and to call out the angelic hosts in judgment. Or he could remain faithful to his calling and drink the bitter cup of obedience. He could tread the path up the hill, carrying his cross, as Isaac bore the wood for his own sacrifice. He could allow himself to be bound to the cross, silently acquiescing, just as Isaac allowed himself to be bound to the altar without a word. As the prophet Isaiah foretold, "As a sheep before her shearers is silent, so he did not open his mouth" (Isa. 53:7). He could look up to heaven and see the knife in the Father's hand poised above him, knowing that for him there would be no last-minute reprieve. For him there would be no substitute, for he was himself the Lamb of God. Whereas Abraham's obedience would lead to a renewal of the blessing, Jesus' obedience would mean embracing the curse. He had to drink the cup of God's wrath to its dregs, if the promise of blessing to Abraham and his descendants was to become a reality. The knife descended. The cup was drained. That is the cost at which we were redeemed. Just as Abraham's willingness to take obedience to the ultimate point demonstrated his love for God beyond a shadow of a doubt, so also God's willingness to take his Son's obedience all the way to the agonies on the cross demonstrated the depth of his love for us beyond a shadow of a doubt. As Paul put it, "He who did not spare his own Son, but gave him up for us all—how will he not also, along with him, graciously give us all things?" (Rom. 8:32).

In comparison, what is demanded of us? For myself and for my loved ones, I must place all my hope beyond the grave. Jesus calls all of us to suffer with him now so that we may be glorified together with him hereafter. We must share in his cross so that we may share in his crown. We must be willing, if necessary, to have all of God's good promises postponed until eternity. God, and God alone, must be enough for us. How hard we find that! How hard it is to wait sometimes! How hard it is to put to death every idol and follow Jesus! But remember this: he was put to death in your place—the spotless Lamb of God for you, a filthy sinner. Our God has provided a Lamb to bear the curse for you and me; let us therefore lay all of our desires on his altar and follow him.

FOR FURTHER REFLECTION

1. How did Abraham respond to God's test?
2. What similarities are there between Isaac and Jesus? In what ways is Jesus' sacrifice different from that of Isaac?
3. From Genesis 22:15–18, what were the results of Abraham's faith and obedience? What were the results of God's decision not to withhold his only Son?
4. Has God ever asked you to sacrifice someone or something you love? What happened? How were you blessed by this experience?
5. Are you ever afraid that God might ask too much of you? What would be too much? What sacrifice would have been too much for God?
6. What was Isaac's response to Abraham's test? From Romans 12:1, how should we be like Isaac?

13

FUNERAL FOR
A FRIEND
(GENESIS 23)

When did you last talk with someone about death? Death has become the ultimate taboo in our society, the one thing we never discuss. It wasn't always that way, however. For example, the Puritan William Perkins wrote a treatise in 1616 entitled *The Right Manner of Dying Well*. Now perhaps past generations sometimes went overboard in discussing death. Some of the books from the Victorian era, telling about children who died wonderful deaths with noble sayings on their lips, rub us the wrong way today. But the Victorians, while afraid even to mention sex, at least talked openly about death.

In our day, we go to the opposite extreme. We talk incessantly about sex, but we try both to hide death and to hide from death. So when it comes, as inevitably it must, we are unprepared to deal with it. We have not learned how to die well. But this chapter has to do with death, the death of Abraham's beloved wife, Sarah. If Genesis 22 showed us a death averted, Genesis 23 shows us a death accepted. Even God's calling and election did not free Abraham and Sarah from that painful reality.

THE DEATH OF SARAH

Sarah died old and full of years, at the age of 127, living in the Promised Land (Gen. 23:2). She did not suffer a long illness. She did not die a tragic death in the prime of life. Yet, in one sense, death is always a tragedy. There is always a sense of sadness and loss on the part of those left behind. There is a sense that this is not how it was supposed to be in the beginning. So Abraham mourned for his wife and wept over her. Mourning is not inappropriate, nor are feelings of sadness at someone's death, even among those of us who expect the resurrection of the dead. Sometimes people give the impression that Christians should be impervious to suffering and should live in an uninterrupted state of happiness. They say, "You've lost your job? Well, praise the Lord anyway," or "Your mother died? You must be glad that she is now with the Lord." We are apparently not supposed to feel any sadness—or at least not let it show. Our unwritten slogan is "Real Christians don't cry."

The Bible, however, has a different perspective. When Jesus saw the sorrow that Martha and Mary were experiencing because of the death of their brother Lazarus, he was deeply moved (John 11:33). When he saw the tomb, he wept too (v. 35), even though he was about to raise Lazarus from the dead. We also grieve when a loved one dies, though not as those who do not share our resurrection hope. The sense of loss at our separation is real, even though it is only a temporary separation.

Abraham and Sarah in many ways demonstrated the principle enunciated in Genesis 2:24, "For this reason a man will leave his father and mother and be united to his wife, and they will become one flesh." Their marriage, in fact, was the first godly one of which we get a glimpse in the Bible. They left home and family behind in a united pursuit of God's calling. Then, many years later, half of that union was called into God's nearer presence. Of course, the fact that they had a godly marriage doesn't mean that they never had any disputes or arguments. We've already looked at one of their strong disagreements (Gen. 21:10–11)! Very likely, there were others that the Scriptures don't mention. Sometimes, too, they led each other astray. Sarah led Abraham off the straight and narrow by suggesting that he take Hagar as a concubine (Gen. 16). The shoe was on the other foot when Abraham hid the fact that he was married to Sarah (Gen. 12 and 20). They were by no means perfect, but they were one flesh, and so Abraham mourned and wept when Sarah was taken from him.

AN ALIEN AND A STRANGER

Death is a time for thinking seriously about eternal things. For Abraham, the death of Sarah underlined the transitory nature of his existence here on earth. So when he came to the Hittites, the people among whom he was then living, he said, "I am an alien and a stranger among you" (Gen. 23:4).

In the Hebrew, the force of what he said is even more pronounced, because the words "an alien and a stranger" come first in the sentence. What he literally said was, "An alien and a stranger am I." Psalm 90 was not yet written in Abraham's time, but he certainly could have identified with the sentiments of Psalm 90:10: "The length of our days is seventy years—or eighty, if we have the strength; yet their span is but trouble and sorrow, for they quickly pass, and we fly away."

It was now some sixty years since God had called him to go to the land that he would give him. Yet here he was, so many years later, still an alien and a stranger, owning no land and having no secure status in the community. He was still just passing through.

BUYING THE FIRSTFRUITS
OF THE INHERITANCE

But the death of Sarah was also a time for Abraham to exercise faith and hope. That is why we have a detailed description of an elaborate ceremony to purchase a field in which Sarah could be buried. If you have found this narrative puzzling, you're not alone. Even some expert commentators have had a hard time with it. For example, the noted German scholar Claus Westermann asks, "Why should a nomad want a piece of property to bury his dead on?"[1] He correctly sees that this is strange behavior, out of character for a nomad—but then he proceeds to miss the point completely!

The strangeness of the behavior is, in fact, precisely the point: Abraham bought a piece of land on which to bury his dead *in faith that one day the entire Promised Land would be his.* Abraham himself would be buried on this spot (Gen. 25:9), as would Isaac and Rebekah, and Jacob and Leah (Gen. 49:29–32). When Joseph was about to die, he gave instructions that his body was not to be buried in Egypt, but to be put in a coffin, so that it could be brought up out of that place and reburied in the Promised Land (Gen. 50:24–26). The field of Machpelah was thus the firstfruits of the Promised Land. It was God's down payment, providing assurance that one day the whole land would be theirs. This aspect of the purchase comes out very clearly in the Hebrew text: Abraham bought an *'achuzzah* (vv. 9, 20). That word carries with it the idea of land as an *inheritance.* Accordingly, in Psalm 2:8 God says to his Anointed One, "Ask of me, and I will make the nations your inheritance, the ends of the earth your possession [*'achuzzah*]." The *'achuzzah* is what God will give to his Anointed One as an inheritance. Strikingly, God had promised to give the land of Canaan to Abraham as an *'achuzzah* in Genesis 17:8—"an everlasting possession," as the NIV translates it. This grave site was the first piece of his promised eternal inheritance.

ENTERING REST

Abraham may still have been an alien and a stranger, but Sarah had entered her rest. It was entirely appropriate that the place of that rest was a piece of the Promised Land—and not simply a borrowed piece of property, but a piece to which they held clear title. In life, the land of Canaan was merely Abraham and Sarah's place of pilgrimage, but, in certain hope of rising again, Abraham wanted to own a piece of it as their resting place. For him and for his wife, no borrowed tomb would suffice. A high price was extracted from him, behind a cloak of polite bargaining, but he considered it worthwhile. Although Ephron the Hittite required him to buy the entire field, not just the cave he had initially requested, and named an almost extortionate price of four hundred pieces of silver, Abraham paid up without demur. But which of them got the better part of the deal? Ephron walked away with a pocket full of silver that he couldn't take with him when he died, but Abraham obtained in symbolic form an inheritance that he could not lose.

Eternal life in God's presence is not cheap; for some, it may cost everything they have and even their very life itself. Nonetheless, it is worth whatever it costs. The departed have no inheritance among the living. But what an inheritance belongs to those who die in the Lord! The whole world is theirs more truly than a rich man owns his mansion. Nothing can separate them from what God has prepared for those who love him, but many things can separate us from our earthly possessions here, no matter how tightly we cling to them or what great deals we strike to increase their quantity.

What is your attitude toward death? Do you hide from

it? Yes, it can often be tragic. Even when it is expected, the sense of loss is still real. We need not deny our feelings and pretend not to be sad. It is appropriate to mourn for our loved ones, just as Abraham mourned for Sarah. Yet we do not mourn as those who mourn without hope. Because Jesus has died for us, and was laid in another cave, we have hope. His tomb was borrowed, not purchased, because he wouldn't be needing it long. On the third day, he rose again as the firstfruits of all those who trust in him. Because of that, death is now the door through which those who believe in Jesus enter life. That reality was still far in the future for Abraham. But by buying this piece of land, Abraham was testifying to his faith in the enduring power of the promises of God. He had faith that not even death could separate him from the love of God. As John Calvin puts it, "While they themselves were silent, the sepulcher cried aloud that death was no obstacle to their entering on the possession of what God had promised."[2]

That is what in former generations would have been called "dying well." It is dying with full assurance of faith that death, while tragic for those who remain behind, is not the end. Rather, it is the door through which you enter into the full measure of the 'achuzzah, the inheritance that God has prepared for those who love him. Are you, like Abraham and Sarah, ready to die well?

FOR FURTHER REFLECTION

1. How did Abraham respond to Sarah's death? How is this a model for us?
2. How should the grief of a Christian differ from that of a non-Christian when loved ones die?
3. How does Abraham describe himself in Genesis 23:4? Why would such a man want to purchase a piece of property?

4. Like Abraham, we possess a "down payment" of the promises of God. What is our down payment, and how does it foreshadow our full inheritance as joint heirs with Christ? Read 2 Corinthians 1:22 for help.

5. What does it mean to you to be an alien and a stranger in this world? How does it affect the decisions you make from day to day?

14

GOD HELPS THOSE
WHO HELP THEMSELVES?
(GENESIS 24)

My father-in-law is a great fan of "Second Hesitations." This is a mythical extra book of the Bible, containing all those well-known sayings that people think are in the Bible, but which are not. A good example is the saying, actually attributable to John Wesley, "Cleanliness is next to godliness." Another "almost biblical" saying is the proverb "God helps those who help themselves." This is many people's motto in life. It was in many ways Abraham's favorite text in his early walk with God. But his life's journey was a process of abandoning that text in favor of a genuine text, "The LORD Will Provide" (Gen. 22:14). We've seen how he was repeatedly faced with the temptation to take shortcuts, to try to help God fulfill the promise. Over the years, he grew in his power to resist it.

A WIFE FOR ISAAC

The temptation to take shortcuts was inevitably most powerful when it seemed most difficult for the promise to be fulfilled. After Sarah's death, Abraham faced another tough situation. Isaac had grown up and needed a wife—not just for the usual reasons, but for the sake of the promise. He needed a wife so that there could be descendants "as numerous as the stars in the sky and as the sand on the seashore" (Gen. 22:17). However, Abraham was living in a foreign country, surrounded by godless Canaanites, the very ones who would be dispossessed by his descendants. Abraham was now well on in years, and Isaac was getting older, too. If Abraham married Isaac to one of the women of the land, that would hardly be a promising scenario for raising up godly offspring. But if he left the Promised Land in order to find Isaac a wife, he would be disobeying God. Either of those options would be a shortcut—an attempt in his own strength to help God fulfill the promise. In this case, Abraham had no direct revelation from God to help him, as he had on some other occasions. He had to follow his conscience, and this time—showing his spiritual growth—his conscience did not lead him astray, but set him on the path of faith.

The path of faith for Abraham was to send his servant on what must have seemed like "Mission Impossible." The servant would have to travel hundreds of miles and find a suitable young woman from Abraham's own people. Then he would have to talk her into coming back with him to the Promised Land to be a wife for someone she had never met. "What if she won't come?" the servant wanted to know. "Do we then take the shortcut of taking Isaac back to the country from which you came?" (Gen. 24:5). "Absolutely not," replied Abraham. His answer was all of faith, fitting for his last recorded words in the Bible.

> The LORD, the God of heaven, who brought me out of my father's household and my native land and who spoke to me and promised me on oath, saying, "To your offspring I will give this land"—

he will send his angel before you so that you can get a wife for my son from there. If the woman is unwilling to come back with you, then you will be released from this oath of mine. Only do not take my son back there. (Gen. 24:7–8)

What Abraham was saying is this: "God will provide a wife, and if he does not do so by this means, we will leave it entirely up to him to fulfill the promise in his own way." No shortcuts would be taken. The doubts and questions were gone now, replaced by a serene faith in God's power and his will to provide. There was no other plan. In the midst of difficult circumstances and an unforeseeable future, faith held firm to two things: God's faithfulness to what he had promised, and the need for obedience.

I've observed over the years that there are two favorite topics that youth groups love to discuss. Those topics are "relationships" and "guidance." Perhaps that is because one of the burning questions of youth is "Who is the right boy/girl for me?" The truth is that whatever your age may be, all you really need to know about guidance can be summed up in this one sentence: God is faithful, so obey him. Whether or not that seems likely to work is not your business. Being faithful to God's revealed will is your business.

MISSION IMPOSSIBLE

So Abraham's servant set out on his impossible task. Arriving at the well of the city, a natural meeting place in the ancient Near East, he devised a test to determine God's will. This is sometimes called "laying out a fleece," after the test devised by Gideon. Gideon put a wool fleece on the threshing floor and asked God to prove his words by causing dew to fall only on the fleece and not on the ground. Then, as confirmation of the test, he asked God for the reverse result the next day (Judg. 6:36–40). Unlike Gideon's fleece, however, the test thought up by Abraham's servant was by no means an arbitrary one. His "fleece" went like this: "May it be that when I say to a girl, 'Please let down your jar that I may have a drink,' and she says, 'Drink, and I'll water your camels too'—let her be the one you have chosen for your servant Isaac" (Gen. 24:14).

He was proposing a test of character, a test of a generous and hospitable spirit. It required someone to be willing to go the extra mile in ministering to a stranger. What is more, his test was bathed in prayer. He was a living example of Proverbs 3:5–6: "Trust in the LORD with all your heart and lean not on your own understanding; in all your ways acknowledge him, and he will make your paths straight."

He didn't ask for a miraculous sign from God. Instead, he sought supernatural guidance in the way it so often comes, through the ordinary events of life.

Abraham knew that it is important to marry only "in the Lord" (see 1 Cor. 7:39). It is only common sense to marry someone who shares the most important thing in your life—and for Christians that is our love for the Lord. But how are we to narrow down that big field? The test that Abraham's servant applied has a more general applicability. We are not to seek for physical beauty, or money, or even the right "chemistry," but rather *character*. The key question we should ask is "Does this person evidence godliness and grace in all of his or her ways?"

AN ANSWERED PRAYER

That's what Abraham's servant was looking for, and he found it in Rebekah. He had barely finished his prayer when the answer appeared in front of his eyes. Rebekah didn't merely do his bidding grudgingly, but hurried to serve him (Gen. 24:18, 20), little knowing the great significance of her actions. She gave him a drink and watered his camels; he responded by giving her costly gifts. As a bonus, she was also "very beautiful" (v. 16). But was she the right one for Isaac? Only when he asked her to what family she belonged, and received the welcome news that she was part of Abraham's wider family, did he permit himself a sigh of relief and of praise: "Praise be to the LORD, the God of my master Abraham, who has not abandoned his kindness and faithfulness to my master" (v. 27). For Isaac, God had provided not merely a lamb, but now also the perfect wife. Abraham's faith in God's provision was fully justified.

In her excitement, Rebekah ran home to Mom with the amazing news, leaving the old man standing at the well. It was left to her brother Laban to go and bring the stranger home. The servant came to Laban's house as an ambassador of good news. But he still wondered whether Laban's household would believe God and act accordingly. Would they entrust Rebekah to a stranger and send her off to a distant land on the strength of God's promise? He would not eat until he received a reply (v. 33). He recounted how God had guided him to Rebekah. He asked her family if they shared in his reading of providence and were willing to entrust her to his care. Their answer was an affirmation of simple faith: "This is from the LORD; we can say nothing to you one way or the other" (v. 50). Like Abraham, they too were from the "God said it; I believe it; that settles it" school of thought. They were apparently his kinfolk at a deeper than physical level.

But note what the servant did *not* say. Even though he was convinced that circumstances had revealed God's will, he didn't try to force his interpretation on Rebekah's family. No, even given the clearest possible guidance on his part, he was willing to put everything to the test of others. He said, in effect, "Here is what it seems to me that the Lord is doing; do you interpret it the same way I do?" He didn't presume to elevate his reading of providence into an infallible authority. Instead, he trusted in God: if this was really God's will, Rebekah's family would give their consent. And they did. They, including Rebekah, saw in this providence the hand of God.

A HAPPY ENDING

Once the decision was made, it was carried out quickly. There was no hesitation, as when Lot was reluctant to leave Sodom. Not even the conventions of Middle Eastern hospitality were allowed to delay the servant's return with Rebekah. He wanted his elderly master to share in the joy of seeing his prayers answered before he died. So Rebekah left with him, not really knowing where she was going or what awaited her there. She went by faith, and was thus a worthy bride for Abraham's son. When her brother and mother asked her if she would go with this man, her answer sparkled with faith. In the Hebrew it is one word: *'elek* ("I will go!") (v. 58).

The story doesn't quite end with Isaac and Rebecca riding off into the sunset together, as it would in a Hollywood film, but it is definitely of the same genre of story endings. The closing scene, depicting their first encounter out in the fields, would look great on the big screen. There were undoubtedly differences between them that would have to be overcome. Certainly they would travel down some difficult paths together. But they had at their disposal the means of overcoming those difficulties because their lives were fundamentally headed in the same direction. They were both led by the same faith in Israel's God. God had brought them together, and their faith in him would sustain them all the days of their life.

Are you looking for guidance? Perhaps you are

tempted to take shortcuts because you can't see any other way out. Remember the basic truths that Abraham had come to learn. God is faithful; we can trust him to provide. Our part is simply to be obedient to his will. Abraham learned that lesson unforgettably on Mount Moriah. There he learned to trust in God's faithfulness against all the odds. There he learned that God doesn't help those who help themselves; he helps those who entrust themselves completely to him. There he learned that the Lord would indeed provide.

We who live after the coming of Jesus have God's faithfulness displayed even more graphically for us on the cross. There God provided his sacrificial Lamb for us, his own beloved Son. God has promised to provide for us everything else we need, too. All that is left for us to do is to return faithful service to God for the faithfulness he has shown to us. In view of what he has done for us, we must say with Abraham, "I will obey, no matter what."

FOR FURTHER REFLECTION

1. Why was Abraham so determined that Isaac should not go back to their home country?
2. How did Abraham's servant go about discerning God's will as to which girl was the right one? How do you go about discerning God's will in such matters?
3. In whom was Abraham trusting for this important provision? What did Abraham believe about God's ability to govern people and circumstances according to his will? What do you believe about God's ability to bring about his will in a sinful world?
4. What are some misunderstandings about finding God's will that are common among Christians today?

5. Through his many experiences with God, Abraham grew strong in faith. How are you growing stronger in faith, and what means is God using to bring about your growth?

15

THE END OF
THE ROAD
(GENESIS 25:1–18)

P eople have always been fascinated by death, wondering what comes next. That is true even today, when we try to hide from death at every opportunity. We all want to know if there is a light at the end of the tunnel—and, if so, if it is the light of an oncoming train, about to run us over and destroy us forever. I once saw a cartoon in *The New Yorker* that showed a man trudging back through a long tunnel. The caption read simply, "Discovering that the light at the end of the tunnel is New Jersey." Our worst nightmare is not that there is nothing after death, but rather that there may be something worse than nothing. For a true New Yorker, what could be worse than spending eternity in New Jersey?

Like all good books, the Bible saves the full resolution of all the reader's questions until the last pages. The closing chapters of the book of Revelation open up in pictorial form the answer to what comes after death. Yet even this early in the biblical story, as we encounter the death of Abraham, we are confronted with the question, "What did Abraham's faith achieve for him? Was it worth all the effort, all the sacrifices, all the pain? Did God indeed fulfill his promises to Abraham?"

The answer given to us in Genesis 25 is "yes and no," or better, "yes and not yet." Yes, God had begun to fulfill his promises to Abraham. But no, those promises were not yet fulfilled completely; he still had to die as he lived, in faith. God had promised Abraham that he would have many descendants (Gen. 13:16; 15:5; 17:2; 22:17) and would be the father of many nations (Gen. 17:4). That promise was fulfilled not simply through Isaac and Ishmael, but also through his children by Keturah, who are listed in the first four verses of Genesis 25. Yet while these were children of Abraham in the physical sense, only Isaac was the child of promise, and therefore only he inherited Abraham's estate (25:5) and along with it the promises made by God to his father. Abraham loved and provided for all his children (v. 6), but there was no longer any confusion in his mind about God's promise. He didn't hedge his bets, giving an inheritance to several of his children, in case one should die or abandon the faith. He trusted the God who said, "It is through Isaac that your offspring will be reckoned" (Gen. 21:12), and acting upon that faith, he made provision for his other children and sent them away.

Abraham lived a long and full life, and then the time came for him to depart. No one is indispensable to God's plan, not even Abraham. His son would take his place in God's plan, to be blessed by God and to be a blessing to the nations (25:11). When Abraham died, he was at peace with God and the world, and ready to depart this earth.

> Altogether, Abraham lived a hundred and seventy-five years. Then Abraham breathed his last and died at a good old age, an old man and full of years; and he was gathered to his people. (Gen. 25:7–8)

His death was in line with what God had promised long before: "You, however, will go to your fathers in peace and be buried *at a good old age*" (Gen. 15:15). The Hebrew phrase in Genesis 25:8 that is translated "at a good old age" is exactly the same as that used in Genesis 15:15. What is more, his funeral was marked by precisely the peace promised in Genesis 15. His sons Isaac and Ishmael buried their differences at least long enough to bury their father together in the cave of Machpelah, where Abraham had earlier buried Sarah (25:9–10). The rest of their lives would be marked by the "in your face" hostility prophesied by the angel of the Lord in Genesis 16:12, which would be passed down to succeeding generations of their children (25:18). For this brief moment, however, their enmity was forgotten as they joined together in the peaceful burial of their father. Here was a man in whose life the promises of God had indeed been fulfilled.

But they had only begun to be fulfilled. Alongside the promises of descendants and peace, there stood the promise of land, a dwelling place for those descendants. But Abraham, like Sarah, died in possession of no more of the Promised Land than he needed for his burial. He had to die in faith, not yet having received the fullness of the promise. His faith therefore stood as a challenge to the Israelites under Moses, as they were about to enter the Promised Land, called to possess it by faith. His faith stood as a challenge to many subsequent generations of Israelites, showing that there was more to God's promise than the possession of a geographical area that they never seemed quite able to fully occupy anyway.

Abraham's faith also stands as a challenge to us today. It is true that we have received greater and more precious promises than Abraham did. Indeed, we have received nothing less than the promised Holy Spirit, poured out upon us and our children, upon all types of people and all classes of society, in a way that the Old Testament saints and prophets could only dream about (Acts 2:17, 38–39).

Yet we too know what it is to see in part, to know in part, to experience in part. Even the fullness of the Holy Spirit that we have received is simply a down payment on what we will one day receive (Eph. 1:14). Like Abraham, we too must live by faith and die by faith, receiving in part, but not yet receiving in full, what God has promised.

That's what it means to live in the reality gap. We live in the real world of joys and sorrows, of successes and failures, of ups and downs. We live in a fallen world, where things and people fail and fall apart. That's reality—and reality is often painful, when those who suffer and die are our loved ones. But the Christian recognizes a reality beyond this reality, a world beyond this world, a story beyond history. He or she knows by faith that the painful reality that we see all around us will one day pass away. It will be replaced by a world in which God will dwell with his people, in which he will wipe away every tear from their eyes, and where there will be no more death or mourning or crying or pain (Rev. 21:3–4). Then we shall see him face-to-face and the reality gap will finally be gone. As Augustine puts it, "There we shall rest and see, see and love, love and praise. Behold what shall be in the end and shall not end."[1] In the meantime, we live, like Abraham, by faith—the faith of those who know that the light at the end of the road is the welcoming presence of Jesus, leading us on to our new home.

> There's a light at the end of the road,
> That can ease my weary mind and loose my
>   load;
> So Jesus shine on brightly through the night,
> And keep me on the high road going right.
>
> 'Cause I know trouble's coming after me,
> And it creeps like a thief in the night.
> I need your loving arms around me,
> To keep my eyes on the light.

There's a stream, I know it flows with life,
I think I'll bathe there today and spend the
	night.
When you wake me touch me softly, take my
	hand once more,
Lead me to the door of my new home.[2]

FOR FURTHER REFLECTION

1. Read Hebrews 11. What did Abraham have in common with the other great men and women described in this passage? How did it make a difference in the way he lived?
2. Which promises did Abraham live to see fulfilled? Which did he hold only by faith when he died?
3. Which of God's promises to you will be fulfilled while you are alive, and which will you inherit when you die?
4. Describe the various ways in which Abraham dealt with his reality gaps. What are your reality gaps? How will you deal with them differently because of what you have learned in this study?
5. How has this study increased your understanding of God, of his great plan of redemption, and of the part we play in that plan?
6. List the three most important truths from the life of Abraham that have made an impact on you.

NOTES

CHAPTER THREE

1 Ambrose Bierce, *The Devil's Dictionary* (New York: Sagamore Press, 1957).
2 Quoted in I. D. E. Thomas, ed., *A Puritan Golden Treasury* (Carlisle, Pa.: Banner of Truth, 1977), 136.

CHAPTER FOUR

1 Albert Hammond and John Bettis, "One Moment in Time" (Bettis Music & Albert Hammond/Warner Chappell Music, 1988).

CHAPTER FIVE

1 Augustus Montague Toplady, "Rock of Ages."
2 Charlotte Elliot, "Just As I Am."
3 Cecil Frances Alexander, "There Is a Green Hill Far Away."

CHAPTER SEVEN

1 Paul Field, "Stony Ground" (Word Music [UK], 1975).

CHAPTER EIGHT

1 Julie Gold, "From a Distance" (Julie Gold/Wing and Wheel Music, 1990).
2 *The Book of Genesis. An Introduction to the Biblical World* (Jerusalem: Magnes, 1990), 80.
3 "To God Be the Glory."

CHAPTER NINE

1   Derek Kidner, *Genesis*, Tyndale Old Testament Commentary (Downers Grove, Ill.: InterVarsity, 1967), 133.

2   "Here Is Love."

CHAPTER THIRTEEN

1   *Genesis 12–36*, trans. J. J. Scullion (Minneapolis: Augsburg, 1985), 376.

2   John Calvin, *Commentaries on the First Book of Moses, Called Genesis*, trans. J. King (Grand Rapids: Eerdmans, 1948), 1:579.

CHAPTER FIFTEEN

1   Augustine *City of God* 22.30.

2   Dan Befus, "The Light at the End of the Road" (Dewey Street Music/ASCAP, 1987).

INDEX OF SCRIPTURE